SEEING RED

SEEING

A STUDY IN CONSCIOUSNESS

RED

NICHOLAS HUMPHREY

THE BELKNAP PRESS OF HARVARD UNIVERSITY PRESS

CAMBRIDGE, MASSACHUSETTS, AND LONDON, ENGLAND

2006

LIBRARY OF CONGRESS CATALOGING-IN-PUBLICATION DATA

Humphrey, Nicholas.

Seeing red : a study in consciousness / Nicholas Humphrey.

　p. cm.—(Mind/brain/behavior initiative)

Includes bibliographical references and index.

ISBN 0-674-02179-7 (hardcover : alk. paper)

1. Consciousness.　I. Title.　II. Series.

BF311.H779　2006

126—dc22　　2005052656

SEEING RED

In 1775 Thomas Reid, a leading light of Scottish philosophy, wrote to the distinguished judge Lord Kames: "I would be glad to know your Lordship's opinion whether when my brain has lost its original structure, and when some hundred years after the same materials are fabricated so curiously as to become an intelligent being, whether, I say, that being will be me; or, if, two or three such beings should be formed out of my brain; whether they will all be me, and consequently one and the same intelligent being."[1]

In 2003 Joe King, an American country and western singer, wrote to me by email: "Hello, my name is Joe King. I am severely disabled, 20 years old. I am 33 inches tall, 40 lbs, 47 broken bones and 6 surgeries. I have been concerned lately that when I die this crippled body might be all I have. My question is. Do u believe consciousness can survive the death of the brain? Is there good scientific evidence for this?"[2]

We do not know Lord Kames's answer to Thomas Reid, and I will not tell you, as yet, mine to Joe King. But these questions, even without answers, reveal something of great significance about the role of consciousness in human lives. People are greatly interested in their own personal survival, which they see very much in terms of the continuity of their own consciousness. Consciousness matters. Arguably, it matters more than anything.

The purpose of this book is to build towards an explanation of just *what* the matter is.

The British psychologist Stuart Sutherland, in his *Dictionary of Psychology* in 1989, gave a curiously sardonic definition of consciousness. "Consciousness is a fascinating but elusive phenomenon; it is impossible to specify what it is, what it does, or why it evolved. Nothing worth reading has been written about it."[3]

You may be surprised—or maybe not—to hear how well this definition has gone down with pundits. A glance at the web (Google, March 2005) shows forty-eight current sites still quoting it with approval. It is clearly a definition that is calculatedly unhelpful. Yet I would say there could be three related reasons why people like it.

And each has some bearing on the ways in which personal consciousness contributes to human self-esteem.

One, the definition taps straight into people's sense of their own metaphysical importance. Consciousness may indeed be an enigma, but at least it is *our* enigma. If there is something so special and even other-worldly about consciousness, then there is surely something special and other-worldly about *us* who possess it.

Two, the definition allows people the satisfaction of being insiders with secret knowledge. It may be difficult for us to describe the nature of consciousness to someone else, but it is not at all difficult for us to observe how it works in our own case. Even if we cannot *say* what it is, nonetheless each of us in the privacy of our own minds *know*s what it is.

Three, the definition puts scientific inquiry in its place. While people are generally happy enough to have science try to explain the way the material world works, many actually do not *want* science to explain the workings of the human mind—at any rate not *thi*s part of the mind. We fear perhaps that consciousness-explained would be consciousness-diminished. So, when a distinguished psychologist pronounces that there is nothing worth reading on the subject, we can rest assured that consciousness is safe for the time being.

You may find you have a sneaking sympathy with each of these opinions. As to the last, I admit that, although I have been engaged in "consciousness studies" for thirty years, I too feel some perverse pride in the fact that consciousness has held out so far against all attempts to treat it as just one more biological phenomenon. I take comfort in the thought that if and when we do finally get a scientific explanation, it will have at least to be an explanation unlike any other.

"A fascinating but elusive phenomenon." You can say that again! But do we perhaps mean fascinating *because* elusive? Would we want it otherwise?

The philosopher Tom Nagel has written, "Certain forms of perplexity—for example, about freedom, knowledge, and the meaning of life—seem to me to embody more insight than any of the supposed solutions to those problems."[4] In a field where so little is agreed or understood, we should expect surprises—and perhaps they will come from the blind-side or even from right behind our backs. Could it be that our very perplexity about consciousness holds the key to why it matters?

It is not always a good idea, in telling a mystery story, to reveal the answer on page four. But I dare say I can tell you just enough to whet your appetite. I shall be arguing that Sutherland's definition of consciousness, born of perplexity, is actually much closer to the mark than ever he intended. If I am right, the last laugh is going to be on Sutherland himself.

Let's look at it again. Sutherland suggests it is impossible to specify what consciousness *is*. But in fact he himself has just alluded to two features that perhaps lie at the very core of what it is: precisely that it is elusive and fascinating.

He suggests it is impossible to specify what consciousness *does*. But in fact he has just provided a perfect example of what is perhaps one of the things it does best: it challenges people to define and make sense of it and brings them face to face with mystery.

He suggests it is impossible to say why consciousness *evolved*. But in fact he has just pointed to something that, as it has played out in history, may perhaps have had a major impact on the way in which human life, as the host to consciousness, is valued.

Then, last, he says that nothing worth reading has been written about consciousness. But perhaps he himself, if only he knew it, has just written something quite unexpectedly worth reading about it: namely, this definition.

All these *perhapses* are tantalizing. But I am going to put them on hold for the time being. There is some other more mundane business (only slightly more mundane) that I want to attend to first. This is to take the generic questions—"What is consciousness? What does it do? Why did it evolve?"—lay them out in good order, and propose a radically new approach to answering them.

There is surely no reason to suppose that answers are *impossible*. But I would certainly agree with Sutherland that there have been a lot of bad answers, and not enough worth reading has been written. So I want to work—rework—this ground with particular care. What I aim to do is to develop a *concept of consciousness* which we, as theorists, can do business with, so that we can see more clearly which problems admit of relatively easy solution and which remain hard.

I should warn you that this reworking of basic issues will take most of the pages (if not the idea space) of the book, with the discussion of the *value* of consciousness coming only at the end. But you need not worry that this means there will not be much of interest in the lead-up.

This book is based on some guest lectures I gave at Harvard University in spring 2004.[5] At the start of the first lecture I put up a screen of plain red light and informed the audience I would spend the next three hours discussing what was going on in their minds as they looked at the red screen. This might indeed have seemed to indicate a rather narrow focus. In fact, my host at Harvard, when I explained in advance what I was planning, wrote back suggesting that perhaps I should attempt something a bit "grander." But, as I hope to show, the discussion that can be raised around a single example of consciousness, "seeing red," goes naturally from grand to grander.

Let me say something about the style in which the book is written. I would like the experience of reading it to be the next best thing to attending a live lecture. Sadly, I shall not be able to draw you into the argument with interactive color images. But I still want it to *sound* like a live lecture. So I shall address you as if we were intimates. And, against all the rules of contemporary editing, I shall make free use of capital letters, italics, and irregular punctuation. A reversion to the grammatical manners of the eighteenth century, perhaps. But no bad thing.

2

The lecture theater has been darkened. And now the projection screen is bathed in bright red light. Something is happening to us as we look at it. The experience of Seeing Red!

What is it like for each of us to be here?

I want to talk you through this, step by step. Phenomenologists, following Husserl, sometimes use the term *epoché,* to mean an attitude where the subject tries to cast aside all ordinary knowledge and preconceptions so as to focus only on what *is.* I am not going to attempt a full-scale phenomenological reduction (I have neither the skill nor the ambition). But I do want to discuss a familiar experience in ways that will certainly not be quite the ways that you are used to.

You may think I am putting things the wrong way round.

You may think I am being unnecessarily pedantic. But let's see how it goes, when we approach things from an unusual direction, and on foot.

So, here we are looking at the red screen—at any rate, here one of us is [Figure 1]. Let's call him S. But you should imagine S to be yourself, as I shall imagine him to be me. What are the basic facts about this situation?

To start with, there is a fact about the screen [Figure 1:a]. The screen, illuminated by the projector, is reflecting what we all agree to call "red light": light with a wavelength around 760 nm, similar to the light that gets reflected from a red object such as a ripe tomato. The screen, in short, is colored red. This, we can say, is an objective fact, which could be confirmed by a physical measuring instrument such as a photometer. It is also an *impersonal* fact. It does not depend on any person's interest or involvement with it. Indeed, this fact about the screen would be the same if we all left the room.

But neither you nor I have left the room. S is here, looking at the screen. And, because S is here, there is now an interesting fact about him [Figure 1:b]. S is doing whatever it amounts to for a person to "see red"—doing it, presumably, somewhere in his brain. This fact about S is also an objective fact. There is every reason to suppose it too could be confirmed by a physical measuring instrument—if not with present technology, then soon enough. What is happening in S's

1

brain is presumably similar to what happens in the brain of any other person who sees red, and its particular signature should be detectable in a high resolution brain scan.

However, this fact about S is a *personal* fact, because it does of course depend on his being here, with his eyes open. It is *his* seeing red. But being personal is only the beginning of what makes this fact remarkable. Far more important is that this fact belongs, among all the facts of the world, to a very special class: namely the class of objective facts that are also *subjective* facts.

S is indeed the *subject* of the *experience* of seeing red. Which means to say S is the *what* of *what* exactly? Being the subject of a visual experience is a complex, layered phenomenon, whose components are not easy to sort out.

There is the story told of an Oxford philosopher who gave lectures one term on *"What do we see?"* He began hopefully with the idea that we see colors, but he abandoned it in the third week and argued that we see things. But that would not do either, and by the end of term he admitted ruefully, "I'm damned if I know what we do see."[1]

Many theorists, before and since, have tried to get a better fix on things than this. In the last hundred years there have been huge advances in the technical sophistication with which psychologists and neuroscientists approach the study of "seeing." Yet the fact remains there is still remarkably little agreement even as to the basic question of what seeing is about.

Just what is contained in the circle of Figure 1:b? Ideas about colors, ideas about things, thoughts, feelings . . . Let's try to explore it, systematically, from the point of view of the person doing the seeing.

The first thing that S, the subject, must surely have to tell us is that there are two very different kinds of things going on. There is a *prop-*

ositional component to his experience and there is a *phenomenal* component.

Let's start with the propositional component. In the process of seeing, S comes to represent *how things are*. He acquires various ideas—beliefs, opinions, feelings—*about what is the case*. Some of these ideas concern the impersonal facts of the world out there, and others, as I shall explain, concern the world in here, the process of seeing itself. In the language of philosophy, these ideas about what's happening are all "propositional attitudes."

In this role as the subject of experience, S is an observer and critic of existing facts. The ideas represent his take on things, he has access to them, and, when occasion arises, they will stand him in good stead for acting on, thinking with, and communicating what he has observed. Still, in this role, S is just that, an observer. The facts as such are at arm's length from him—there to be observed.

But seeing also has a phenomenal component. In the process of seeing, S also brings into being a state of "phenomenal consciousness." In particular, S creates visual sensations, with a striking qualitative feel to them. In the language of philosophy again, he generates "visual qualia."

In this role as the subject, S is not merely an observer of what is already the case, he is the active author of something quite new. What's more, these new facts, these sensations, are no longer at arm's length from him—instead, in an important sense, they *are him,* they constitute the very essence of his subjectivity. Yet despite being so vivid and so central, his sensations are not *about* anything. So, unlike propositional attitudes, they are not readily thinkable, let alone communicable.

But this is already getting too abstract and theoretical. We should focus in, as I said we would, on the particular experience of seeing red. Most discussions of seeing in conventional textbooks take the propositional components to be the major issue, and get round to considering the phenomenal component only as an afterthought (or not at all). But I want to reverse this and begin (as I mean to go on) with the part of the experience that I would say is, for the subject, by far the most dramatic.

When S looks at the screen, he does something truly remarkable (in fact so remarkable that, if he were not so breezily familiar with it, he might rub his eyes in disbelief every time it happens): he generates that particular state of consciousness he will call *having a red sensation.*

This sensation is clearly something *he* creates. Something that does not exist before he looks at the screen, and will vanish when he closes his eyes. Some *thing* indeed, a new fact of his own making. So, we can show it in the diagram [Figure 2:b] as a fact—part of the fact about S—of equivalent status to the fact about the screen [Figure 2:a].

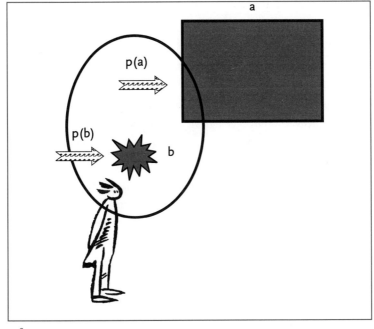

2

Just what kind of fact this is we shall have to discover. But let me anticipate and suggest now (as I shall elaborate later in the book) that having a red sensation has something of the character of a *bodily action,* perhaps an *expression.* At any rate, it is an active first-person response to being stimulated with red light. And, to bring this out, let's give a special active name to what S is doing here: *redding.*

This sensation, this redding, is the centerpiece of *what it's like to be S at this moment.* As its author, S experiences it immediately, in the making—or so it seems. And yet, even though S is doing it, just what it is he is doing will be more than he can fully *say.* Indeed, as he tries to think about it, he will find the redding arrives in consciousness before he can even begin to put his mind to it and extends deeper than he can put his mind to (even given all time in the world).

It is hard to find the right metaphor to express this signal difficulty. The painter Bridget Riley has written about sensation, "For all of us, colour is experienced as something—that is to say, we always see it in the guise of a *substance*."[2] Her choice of the word "substance," with its Platonic overtones, is revealing—as if she is suggesting that sensation belongs to the world of substantial Platonic forms of which we can communicate only the pale *shadow.*

Helen Vendler, the Shakespearean critic, writing of another art form, has said, "I assume that a poem is not an essay, and that its paraphrasable propositional content is merely the jumping-off place for its real work."[3] I think we all have the hunch that sensations likewise have real work to do, of a sort to which verbal descriptions cannot do justice. The question of what this real work is will have to be a major issue for later in the book.

Now, in certain circumstances, this, the redding, could be the sum of it, all there is to the experience of seeing red. Suppose, for example, that, instead of actively looking at the screen, S were to be lying on his back under the sun, with eyes closed, thinking about something else, with light percolating through his blood-shot eyelids. Then quite likely, apart from the redding, there would be nothing further to report.

But this is not S's situation now. Here S is, actively interested in seeing. And now the *propositional components* to his experience are kicking in: ideas—beliefs, opinions, feelings—*about* what's the case. S is the subject of these ideas. But his role now is more that of a reporter than an author. And, because the ideas are indeed *about* something, he will be able to describe them to us relatively easily.

There are two facts that potentially interest S: the fact of the screen [Figure 2:a] *and* the fact of the sensation [Figure 2:b]. But these are very different kinds of fact, and S may find his attitudes toward them taking different forms and directions. His ideas *about* the facts are labeled in Figure 2:p(a) and p(b), respectively. Although in most circumstances S is likely to give the fact of the screen priority, he will be able to switch attention relatively easily between one and the other. And since it is sensation that we have already brought into focus, let us begin our analysis with having S pay attention to sensation.

I said that, at the level of phenomenal consciousness, S experiences the sensation immediately, in the very act of doing it. This immediate experience does not, as such, constitute a propositional attitude, because it is not in its own right about anything. However, S, the subject, can certainly have ideas about the sensation [Figure 2:p(b)]—even if what they amount to is merely the "paraphrasable propositional content" of what it's like.

The first and most obvious thing S will surely have to say about the sensation, the redding, is that it is a *visual* sensation. Which is to say no more or less than that it has the style S recognizes as typical of those sensations he creates in response to light at his eyes, as distinct from the sensations he creates in response, for example, to sound at his ears or odors at his nose.

S will say that, as a visual sensation, it fills a patch of his visual field with the presence of color. He can describe the shape and location of this patch: roughly rectangular, upper right quadrant. And he can classify the color of it as bright red.

Now, you may question what S means by saying that the sensation he is creating has this shape and this color. It can hardly be the case that the activity of redding, this fact, b, has these physical properties—that the redding as such is located in his visual field or is colored red. We can agree. But what he means, we may guess, is that the sensation is somehow tracking the light stimulus to which it's a response. Indeed, S has only to experiment a little—by rolling his eyes, blinking, and so on—to discover that certain properties of the sensation map precisely onto properties of the *retinal image at his eyes.* As the image changes, so does the sensation. So, when he says the sensation has shape and color, he is really saying the sensation has properties that *represent* precisely these properties of the image.

We shall see later just what kind of representation this may be. Still, one thing that is obvious immediately is that the sensation is by no means a simple copy of the retinal image as a physical fact. For it is strikingly obvious to the subject that the sensation, the redding, has a *quality* and a *valency*—subjective psychical properties—which the image as such could hardly have. The sensation represents not just the red light at his eyes but his interaction with this stimulus. And because of this, S will feel the sensation matters to him; he will mind about it.

The painter Kandinsky wrote, "Color is a power which directly influences the soul. Color is the keyboard, the eyes are the hammers, the soul is the piano with many strings."[4] But even a single color sensation, such as this redding, playing all on one note, can have considerable impact—not only in human beings but in animals as well.

In research of my own with rhesus monkeys, I showed that they have strong and consistent emotional responses to colored light. When, for example, a monkey is put in a chamber bathed in red light, it becomes anxious and fidgety; when the chamber is bathed in blue, it becomes relatively calm. Given the choice, monkeys strongly prefer a blue chamber to a red one.[5]

Human beings (and, for that matter, pigeons too) generally respond to colored light in similar ways.[6] They describe the sensation of red as strong, hot, exciting, and disturbing. Red light has been found to induce physiological symptoms of arousal, while blue light has the opposite effect, and this is true even in babies as young as fifteen days. Subjects feel warmer in red rooms than in blue, time seems to pass faster, reaction times go down.

In a book on *Colour for Architecture,* Tom Porter and Byron Mikellides relate that "Michelangelo Antonioni, the Italian film director, made an interesting observation during the making of his first colour film, *The Red Desert.* While shooting industrial scenes on location in a factory, he painted the canteen red in order to invoke a mood required as background to the dialogue. Two weeks later he observed that the factory workers had become aggressive and had begun to fight amongst themselves. When the filming was completed the canteen was repainted in a pale green in order to restore peace and so that, as Antonioni commented, 'The workers' eyes could have a rest.'"[7]

It is true that people, unlike monkeys, sometimes seek out red light when the mood takes them. But this may be for the very reason that it stirs them up. Isaac Newton, as one remarkable example, furnished his London house entirely in crimson—a "crimson mohair bed," with "crimson bed-curtains," "crimson mohair hangings," a "crimson settee"—almost as if he were trying, by living in this "atmosphere of crimson," to ensure he lived up to his reputation for being irritable.[8] Henri Matisse, when painting a picture of his studio—and wanting to convey not so much the physical reality as the highly charged emotional atmosphere he associated with it—changed the color of the walls in the picture several times, until he settled finally on *The Red Studio*.

It is important to note that these aesthetic attitudes to color are primarily attitudes to the quality of the sensation that colored light induces *in the subject*, not to the fact that some *thing* has the colored surface it has. That's to say, when S finds red light exciting, for example, it is his own phenomenal experience, the redding, that he judges exciting, and not the fact that the screen is colored red.

I shall discuss evidence later that directly supports the contention that *sensation is what matters*. But I may mention now one finding with my monkeys that bears on it.[9] The monkeys showed a strong preference for being in the presence of a blue screen as against a red one when the screen was blank and featureless. However, this preference completely disappeared when there were interesting things on the screen to look at. In the first situation, the monkeys had nothing to attend to but their own sensations, and so they had a preference for the sensation of blue over the sensation of red; but in the second situation, where their attention was drawn out to the external world and away from their own responses, it seems they now had no preference for *things in the world being blue* over *things in the world being red.*

So, now, at last, what about the subject's propositional attitudes to the screen as a fact of the world? In continuing our step-by step analysis, let us now have S switch his attention away from the fact of sensation and direct it to this other fact of the red screen. When he looks at the red screen, what ideas does he form about it [Figure 2:p(a)]? In familiar language, what does he *perceive?*

S will say, no doubt, that he perceives that there is indeed a screen out there, that it has such and such a size, shape, and location in external space, and that, yes, the screen is colored red, the color of a ripe tomato.

No problem now with what S means by saying that *the screen* has a shape and color. He is not now describing some mental process of his own in these terms, something that merely correlates with or represents the screen; he is describing the screen as such.

But, just to the extent that S is now perceiving a fact of the world and not a fact about himself, his ideas about the screen will be markedly different from his ideas about sensation. Crucially, S perceives this fact of the screen as the *impersonal* fact it is. It's true that it is he, S, who is doing the perceiving, but the thing his perception is *about* is the screen out there in the world—he does not perceive it as red *for him.*

Indeed, so little is S himself involved with this external fact that he does not even perceive it as red *for his eyes.* Unlike the fact of the red sensation, which is a fact bound up with how S himself is responding to light and so is *essentially seeing-related,* the fact of the screen being red is in no way dependent on his seeing it. So, in principle S might be able to arrive at the very same idea by means of a different sense organ, without using his eyes at all. Perhaps it might even be enough if S were to have someone he trusts tell him.

An apparatus, called vOICe, has recently been developed for helping blind people to see using their ears rather than their eyes.[10] The subject wears a helmet with a video camera mounted on it, coupled to a light-to-sound translation program, with headphones to receive the sound image. The device has the potential to map visual scenes to "soundscapes" in an analog way. Future versions will likely code color as a continuous extra dimension of the soundscape. However, as of now, when it comes to "seeing color," the device takes a short-cut and *says* the word RED! As the user's manual explains, when you activate a color identification button, "the talking color probe speaks the color detected in the center of the camera view. Now you know whether the apple you are about to eat is yellow, green or red, and you can check the dominant colors of your clothing."

Suppose S himself were blind and (unknown to us) were using this device to look at the screen. Though S would presumably not claim he was having a red visual sensation, he could still report accurately that he perceives the screen is colored red.

Maybe you think what I am suggesting here is unrealistic: namely, that a person's belief about the color of an external object may quite well be "sensory modality-neutral." But then consider the discovery recently made by child psychologists that three-year-old children sometimes really do not seem to know by what sensory route they have come by their beliefs about the properties, including the color, of objects in their environment. Put a green squishy ball in a three-year-old child's hand and ask her what color it is, and she will look at it and say green; ask her whether it is hard or soft, and she will squeeze it and say soft. But now put it in a bag and ask her what she would *have to do* either to find out what its color is or to find out whether it is hard or soft—would she have to put her hand in and feel it or would she have to take a look?—and she will likely say she does not know the answer.[11]

Given the possibility of perceptual beliefs being free-floating, as it were, it is of great interest that linguists have recently drawn attention to the existence of human languages where the rules of grammar demand that statements about belief carry explicit reference to how the belief was acquired. For example, in the South American Tariana language, a statement such as "I know it's raining" has to be glossed with a suffix indicating how the speaker knows it—"I know it's raining visual" (that is, I see it), as against "I know it's raining aural" (I hear it). The requirement that the information source is identified is called "evidentiality."[12]

Let's return to the case of S looking at the screen. He perceives that the screen is colored red. But he does not perceive this as a fact with any intrinsic connection to himself or to his eyes. So, now, what attitudes if any will he have toward this perceived fact at an affective level? Will he *mind* about the color of things out there in the world?

As we have already discussed, the answer is most likely no. This is not to say that the impersonal facts of color do not matter to anyone in any circumstances. But they certainly do not matter in the way colored sensations do. If I shut my eyes, I still have the perceptual knowledge that the screen is colored red, but I do not find the knowledge as such loud, hot, disturbing, exciting. Maybe it is true that, if I were blind, I "could use the vOICe apparatus to check the dominant color of my clothing." But would I care?

Suppose Newton, wearing a blindfold, had been obliged to make do with a voice telling him that his curtains and settees were colored CRIMSON. Would his expensive furnishings have had any of the desired effects?

Let us take stock of where we are. We have listed three separate components of the experience of looking at the screen:

- S gets to have a red sensation, b
- S gets to feel he is having this red sensation, p(b)
- S gets to perceive the screen is red, p(a)

But I want to draw attention also to an important fourth component. In doing all this, S gets to experience himself *as an experiencer.*

The logician Gottlob Frege (following on from Kant much earlier) nicely stated the general principle that lies behind this: that wherever there is subjective experience there *has to be a subject.* "It seems absurd to us that a pain, a mood, a wish should rove about the world without a bearer, independently. An experience is impossible without an experient. The inner world presupposes the person whose inner world it is."[13]

Frege is usually taken to be suggesting that the person has to be there first. But clearly it can be the case—and surely it often is—that we understand the situation to be the other way around. That's to say, it is our experience of the inner world that confirms the existence of the person.

Hold on to this. I think it is of key importance. Indeed, I give you notice that I shall conclude this book by arguing that this may be the key that unlocks the deepest mysteries of consciousness. But for now I shall simply note that sensation has a special role to play here. At the same time as S *makes sensation,* he may well feel that *sensation makes him.* And this making of him is something about which he is bound to have strong views on a rather different meta-level. S will almost certainly *like* being the kind of entity that has such remarkable conscious experiences. He will be interested, proud to be "the person whose inner world it is." As Lord Byron wrote in a letter to his future wife: "The great object of life is sensation—to feel that we exist even though in pain."[14]

So, let's add this to the list. In looking at the screen:

- S gets to have a red sensation, b
- S gets to feel he is having this red sensation, p(b)
- S gets to perceive the screen is red, p(a)
- S gets to experience his Self

Now, I would say that these four points just about cover it. And this might be as far as we need take the analysis for the time being—if it were not for one highly significant circumstance. We must not forget that S, in the lecture theater, is looking at the screen *in the presence of other people.* And this social context introduces a whole new set of issues.

The Roman dramatist Terence famously remarked: "I am a man, and I think nothing human alien to me." Which grand sentiment, taken to the local level, means S is—he cannot but be—interested in what is going through *your* mind [Figure 3]. No account of S's experience will be complete unless it takes in his experience of *your* looking at the screen.

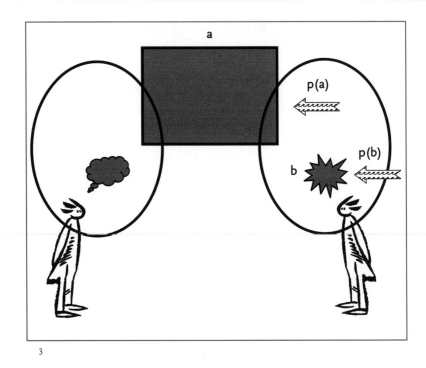

3

S's "theory of mind," as psychologists call it, may be based either on his putting himself imaginatively in your place (a "simulation" theory of mind) or on his thinking it through on some more abstract deductive level (a "theory" theory of mind). But, either way, the upshot is: S presumes that *you too are seeing red*.

Ah, but *what* does S presume about your seeing red? And how confident can he be that he has got it right? Let's go over the four things we have just discussed (though now maybe we should take them in a different order).

To start with, S supposes that when you look at the screen, you get to learn about the same impersonal fact of the world as he does. That's to say, he supposes you too perceive that the screen is colored red, the color of a ripe tomato [Figure 3:p(a)]. It's true, S might be mistaken about this. Unknown to him, you might be color-blind, so that you see everything as black and white. Or you might have a rare condition called color agnosia, in which the color-classifying areas of your brain no longer function properly.

However, this is something S should be able to check out relatively easily. All he need do is ask you. Since S's perception of the screen's color and your perception of the screen's color do concern precisely the same impersonal fact, a, then unless there is indeed something wrong with you (or wrong with him), he and you will openly agree on it. If it turns out that you do not agree—if, perhaps, you say the screen is the color of a blueberry while he says it is the color of a to-mato—S could appeal to an objective physical measuring instrument to decide who is right. Assuming the instrument confirms *his* perceptual judgment, then S might well want to *correct* you.

But now let's move closer in on *what it's like* for you. Granted that you do perceive the screen to be colored red, S no doubt imagines that you get to have much the *same phenomenal experience* as he does. He believes you too are creating a *red sensation;* you are redding [Figure 3:b]. Again, it's true S might be mistaken about this. Unknown to him, you might have taken consciousness-altering drugs, so that the sensation you are creating is not the normal one. Or you might even have been *born* to do things differently, so that all your life the sensation you create when you look at a red screen has perhaps been more like the sensation S creates when he looks at a blue screen: when S engages in redding, perhaps you engage in blueing.

However, now it is by no means so straightforward to check this out. S's sensation and your sensation are two separate facts, not the same one. They are personal facts inside his and your respective brains, and there is as yet no instrument for objectively measuring and comparing them.

S certainly cannot hope to resolve the question by asking you straight out, since presumably you will not be able to speak to the essential nature of your experience any more than he can. Nonetheless, S may still think it reasonable to *try* to compare notes on this as well. For he may well assume that you—like he—do have at least a limited degree of propositional access to the sensation you are creating [Figure. 3:p(b)]. You too *feel* that you are having it, and you should be able to tell or show him something of *what* you are feeling.

Given S's assumption that you and he are in fact doing something similar, he can expect for a start that you will tell him you are having a *visual* sensation, and not, say, an auditory one (assuming, that is, that you are not someone who is blind and using the vOICe apparatus!). But more than this, S can expect you to agree with him about what the sensation does for you on an affective level—that it is a strong, hot color, say.

Suppose, however, you surprise him and claim that your sensation, even though visual, is actually cool and calm, like bathing in an alpine lake. In this case S will not of course want to *correct* you. Instead, he may reasonably conclude that your sensation is actually *not* like his: that perhaps you really are blueing when he is redding. Why not? It's your mind. You might, as we said, even have been born that way.

My monkeys all had astonishingly similar attitudes toward color. In straight preference tests, all ten animals I studied preferred blue to green to yellow to red—which strongly suggests a species-wide genetic basis for it. Most human beings have similar preferences if tested under standard conditions. And yet not all do. Chris McManus, in a study of people's preferences for colored cards, involving 54 people, each making 256 paired comparisons, found that while 70 percent of his subjects consistently preferred blue/green hues to yellow/red hues, a significant subgroup of 20 percent showed a distinctly different pattern, consistently preferring yellow/red to blue/green.[15] Although we should not make too of this, let's allow that is thought-provoking.

I hasten to point out that even if S and you agree on everything there is to say about what it is like to be having the sensation—modality, affect, whatever—this will still not be a guarantee that his and your phenomenal experiences are the same in *all* respects. Given everybody's lack of propositional access to some of the essential qualities of the experience, there could be differences between people that do not show up in anything at a behavioral level.

It is fair to say that any such hidden differences, if they exist, cannot be all that important, certainly not life-changing. But they could be real and nontrivial nonetheless. I have suggested before now the analogy of two people, A and B, who each has a private box with a clock in it, which he can use to tell the time.[16] Their clocks are identical except for one peculiar feature: namely, that while the hands on A's clock turn in a clockwise way, the hands of B's turn in an anticlockwise way. When A and B read their clocks, they agree about what time it is, about the rate time is passing, and so on. It seems the direction of rotation is a difference that does not make a difference. And yet it is a difference to which we can certainly assign meaning—and even significance.

We should acknowledge, then, that S, looking at the screen with you, ought to accept that there may be—and quite likely are—some unverifiable differences between him and you. There has to be wiggle-room, even if not much, for totally private idiosyncrasy.

Still, let's be clear that, even if S cannot be entirely sure about what it's like for you, he can be sure enough of *something:* namely, that you *are* (or, as an outside possibility, *are not*) having a visual sensation of some kind. For there is every reason to believe that if you were not to be having any sensation at all, you would be the first to know it—and to say it.

There is a rare condition that occurs after damage to the visual cortex of the brain, called blindsight (of which I shall have much more to say in the next chapter), where it seems the patient really does lack all visual sensation, even though he is still able to perceive—at least to make accurate *guesses* about—certain features of the external world, including color. Let's suppose, against the odds, that you are someone with blindsight. Could S possibly fail to miss this crucial truth about you? Not if he takes the simple step of asking you. For, as a matter of fact, the absence of sensation is something of which the blindsight patient is all too well aware: indeed, typically, he himself will loudly protest that, however good his perceptual guesses, *consciously* he is blind.

Let's suppose, which is even more unlikely, that you are someone who was *born* to be someone who lacks all visual sensations—a kind of visual zombie.[17] Perhaps, since you have never known the difference, you would not spontaneously remark on it, in the way the blindsight patient does. Nevertheless, I do not think it would take much questioning to find it out.

To return to reality, S can—and presumably will—have ways of discovering that you are not a zombie. I will freely admit, for my own part, I am glad of this. I have already claimed that S (but I am really talking about myself) *likes* having sensations, S likes being conscious. But I am equally sure that S also likes consciousness in *you*. The last thing S wants to believe is that he is the only Self there is.

The British comedian Stephen Fry wrote a novel in which his hero toyed with the opposite opinion: "They don't exist, he kept repeating to himself as they rattled up the A1 motorway. Other people don't exist . . . It's all just a clever way of testing me. There's no one in these cars and lorries driving south. There can't be that many individual souls. Not souls like mine. There isn't room. There can't be."[18] Yet, if anyone really believed this, he would be unutterably lonely. I confess I find it upsetting even to imagine that my dog might be a zombie.

There, that will do. This takes the phenomenological analysis as far as we need go for the moment. Here are some of the issues and distinctions that have come to light.

1 phenomenal experience / propositional attitudes
2 sensation / perception
3 values / facts
4 first-person / third-person
5 theory-theory of mind / simulation-theory of mind
6 being there / emptiness

Ludwig Wittgenstein teasingly remarked, "We find certain things about seeing puzzling, because we do not find the whole business of seeing puzzling enough."[19] I think we can claim the whole business is getting to be plenty puzzling. It is time to turn to the question of what lies behind it.

3

Why do we human beings experience the world in this surprisingly complex way? What are the structural and functional reasons for it? What is their evolutionary history? What, in particular, is the evolutionary history of *consciousness?*

In the world at large, the term consciousness has both broad and narrow uses. If our subject S were to say that in looking at the red screen he is "consciously seeing red," he might possibly be referring to any or all of the components of the experiences we have identified: "I'm consciously having a red sensation," "I'm conscious that the sensation is red," "I'm conscious that the screen is red," "I'm conscious of being me," even "I'm conscious of you being you."

But we need not be shy of declaring an overriding interest in just one of these: *phenomenal consciousness.* As we go on, we shall touch on questions to do with a variety of related issues. But at heart will be the big one, the hard one, the challenge that makes so many throw up their hands: What is phenomenal consciousness and how did it evolve? Or, as we can now reframe this: What is *creating a sensation*, what makes it *like this to be the subject of it*, and why does it *matter*?

Stuart Sutherland, as we saw, was saying thirty years ago that no student of consciousness has had any good ideas. And, for the cynics, nothing much changes. The philosopher Jerry Fodor offered this as his considered opinion in 2004: "Nobody has the slightest idea what consciousness is, or what it's for, or how it does what it's for (to say nothing of what it's made of)."[1] Suppose Fodor were to be here with us right now in front of the red screen. He would, I am sure, be happy to be more specific: "Nobody has the slightest idea what the experience of creating a red sensation is, or what it's for, or how it does what it's for (to say nothing of what it's made of)."

Then, with this as the new challenge, let's get going. And let's try, to begin with, to find out more about what *sensation* is. As we do so, however, it is important that we take on board a kind of philosophical health-warning. We should recognize that, even if sensation is the vehicle and occasion of phenomenal consciousness, the discovery of what sensation *is* will not necessarily tell us why what it is *is conscious*. Indeed, we may have to dig still deeper before we understand why sensation's being whatever it is brings with it the extra feature that somehow lifts ordinary sensory experience into the realm of phenomenally rich conscious sensory experience—the mysterious extra feature that the philosopher Daniel Dennett has (skeptically) dubbed "the factor X."[2]

It is possible that, as we close in on what sensation is, this X factor will simply fall into our lap. But it may not. We can only try our luck.

In a typical example of seeing, there are at least three things going on [refer again to Figure 2]:

- the having of a sensation, b
- the feeling of having this sensation, p(b)
- the perception of a fact in the external world, p(a)

Even if our main goal is to explain the nature of sensation, it is clear we had better start by asking how these three components are related. Indeed, on the basis of my own and others' failures here, I can promise that unless we do this first—and get it right—we shall remain as stuck in the mire as everyone else has been.

So, I have to tell you the bad news. Which is that, after several hundred years of philosophical and psychological discussion, the relation between these three different components of sensory/perceptual experience is really not properly understood.

In 1785 the philosopher Thomas Reid was the first to draw explicit attention to the multilayered character of sensory experience: "The external senses have a double province—to make us feel, and to make us perceive. They furnish us with a variety of sensations, some pleasant, others painful, and others indifferent. At the same time they give us a conception and an invincible belief of the existence of external objects."[3]

Reid's own favorite example was the case of smelling a rose: "The agreeable odour I feel, considered by itself, is merely a sensation. It affects the mind in a certain way; and this affection of the mind may be conceived, without a thought of the rose or any other object. This sensation can be nothing else than it is felt to be. Its very essence consists in being felt; and when it is not felt it is not . . . Perception [by contrast] has always an external object; and the object of my perception, in this case, is the quality in the rose that I discern by the sense of smell."[4]

In the terms we have established in the previous chapter, when S smells a rose [Figure 4],

- S gets to have an olfactory rosy sensation, s
- S gets to feel his having of this rosy sensation, $p(s)$
- S gets to perceive the rose has a rosy smell, $p(r)$

The question is how these three things are connected. Reid himself proposed a simple answer: namely, that sensation provides the

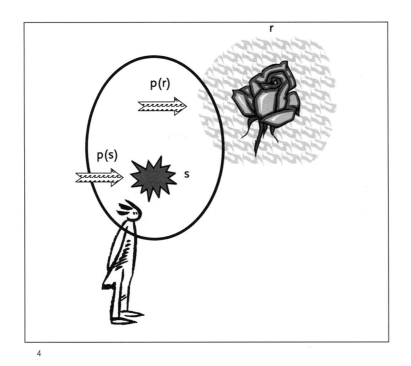

4

evidence on which perception is based. That's to say, the several components lead on, one to another, in a serial way. Thus, Reid continued: "Observing that the agreeable sensation is raised when the rose is near, and ceases when it is removed, I am led by my nature, to conclude some quality to be in the rose, which is the cause of this sensation. This quality in the rose is the object perceived."[5]

This idea of a serial chain from sensation to perception might seem to make perfect sense [see Figure 5].

1 The external object, a, transmits a stimulus to the sense organ, a'.
2 S creates a sensation, b, as some kind of low-level copy of this sensory stimulus.
3 S reads the properties of the sensation, p(b).
4 Finally S uses this reading as a basis for reconstructing the facts of the external world p(a).

The final step need not of course involve deliberate deduction. Rather, it could, as Reid says, be a case of being "led by nature to conclude," or, as later philosophers would call it, a case of "unconscious inference."

It is an old and familiar way of picturing things, and one which still informs many lay people's understanding of perception. But the problem is that we have long known—at any rate, psychological science has long known—that this simply cannot be how it works.

For a start, we know there are a variety of situations in which the subject may be able to make accurate perceptual judgments about external objects even though the stimulus is too weak or too brief to give rise to any sensation at all—the phenomenon called "subliminal perception." But, more tellingly, the subject may still be able to make accurate judgments even when the capacity for sensation has been totally disabled. The paradigm example of this is the phenomenon of blindsight, which was mentioned briefly in the previous chapter.

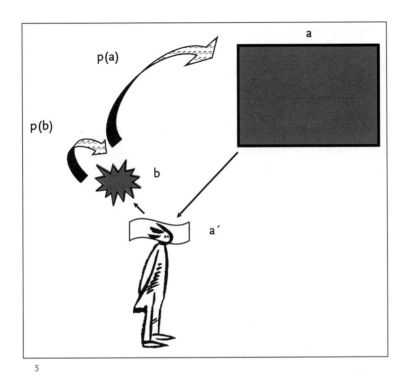

5

Since blindsight will figure prominently in the coming argument, let me give some history.

The first hint I myself had that a condition like blindsight might exist came through research with a brain-lesioned monkey, begun when I was a PhD student at Cambridge University in 1967.[6] A monkey in my supervisor Larry Weiskrantz's laboratory, named Helen, had undergone a surgical operation which removed the primary visual cortex at the back of her brain, with the purpose of discovering more about the role the cortex plays in normal vision. The operation had been done in 1965, and during the following two years the monkey had seemed to be almost completely blind. However, I had reasons for thinking this might not be the whole story.[7] And so, one week when I had time on my hands and the monkey was not involved in Weiskrantz's research, I decided to find out more.

Over several days I sat by the monkey's cage and played with her. To my delight, it soon became clear that this blind monkey was sometimes *watching* what I did. For example, I would hold up a piece of apple and wave it in front of her, and she would clearly *look,* before reaching out to try to get it from me. As the game continued, she soon transformed herself from a monkey who sat around listlessly, gazing blankly into the distance, into one who was interested and involved in vision again.

I persuaded Weiskrantz to let me go on working with Helen. Over the next seven years I took her with me to Oxford, and then back to Cambridge, to the Department of Animal Behaviour at Madingley. I became her tutor on a daily basis. I took her out on a leash in the fields and woods at Madingley. I encouraged her and coaxed her, trying in every way to help her realize what she might be capable of. And slowly but surely her sight got better. Eventually she could, for example, run around a room full of obstacles, picking up crumbs off the floor. Anyone who was unaware that she had no visual cortex could well have assumed she had completely normal vision.

Yet I was pretty sure her vision was not normal. I knew her too well. We had spent so many hours together, while I continually wondered what it was like to be her. And, although I found it hard to put my finger on what was wrong, my sense was that she still did not *really believe* that she could see. There were telling hints in her behavior. For example, if she was upset or frightened, she would stumble about as if she was in the dark again. It was as if she could only see provided she did not try too hard.

In 1972 I wrote an article for the *New Scientist,* and on the front cover of the magazine they put the headline, under Helen's portrait, "a blind monkey that sees everything" [Figure 6]. But this headline surely was not right. Not *everything.* My own title for the paper inside the magazine was "Seeing and Nothingness," and I went on to argue that this was a kind of seeing of which we had never before had any inkling.[8]

With a monkey, who could not describe her inner world, there seemed no way of knowing what her experience was really like. To find out, we would need evidence from human beings, and at that time there were no human cases comparable. What evidence there was suggested that people with similar brain damage would *not* recover vision. I wrote: "When people suffer extensive damage to the

30 March 1972

Weekly 12p

new scientist

Australia 35 cents/
Canada 60 cents/
New Zealand 35 cents/
South Africa 30 cents/
USA (by air) 90 cents/
BF 25/FF 3/DM 2.50/
hfl 1.50/skr 3.00/

A blind monkey that sees everything

6

visual cortex it is said that their blindness is total and permanent. Perhaps with a more flexible definition of vision, it will yet be discovered that there is more to seeing than has so far met either the clinician's or the patient's eye."

Then, within a couple of years, Weiskrantz, spurred on by what we had found with Helen, moved the research to a new level by showing that a human patient with extensive damage to the visual cortex could be coaxed, like the monkey, into demonstrating a significant degree of vision in the blind part of his visual field. But now, with this human patient, it was possible to have him tell the researchers what it was like for him. And, to everyone's astonishment it turned out that, yes, this was indeed a kind of *unconscious vision.*

The patient believed he was blind, and *reported that he was having no visual sensation,* and yet he could still *guess* the position and shape of objects.[9] What's more, it later turned out that he could also accurately guess colors. So this patient, were he here now, with the screen in the blind part of his field, though he would say he had no red sensation, could still tell us that the screen is colored red.[10]

The reality of blindsight has now been confirmed with a dozen or more patients. I shall want to come back and mine it for further revelations later. But the immediate point is this: the existence of blindsight is as good a proof as we could ask for that visual perception does not necessarily *have to* involve sensation. If the serial pathway of Figure 5, from sensation to perception, exists at all, it clearly cannot be the only pathway. There must be an independent pathway that does not go via sensation, which can be used when sensation is not present.

In that case, however, what reason is there to suppose the serial pathway does exist at all? Surely, the alternative possibility we should consider is that perception proceeds independently of sensation even when sensation *is* present. What kind of evidence might possibly support this much more radical suggestion?

Suppose that the process that creates sensation, rather than breaking down completely, were to malfunction and generate a distorted and misleading copy of the stimulus. If perception does depend on sensation when it is present, this malfunction would seem bound to have knock-on effects on perception. However, if perception is relatively independent of sensation, this malfunction might leave perception more or less unscathed.

Are there such cases? Yes, in fact there are a range of cases where—as a result of drugs or brain damage—patients report major changes going on at the level of sensation. And the remarkable thing is that, in some cases at least, *the patient's perception of the external world does remain apparently unaffected.* Thus, for example, patients with damage to the parietal cortex of the brain sometimes experience a curious condition—a variety of metamorphopsia—where their visual fields appear to be in flux, swelling, or contracting, or changing color, even when the external world is unchanging. Yet, in the midst of such sensational chaos, the patient may actually have little if any trouble in getting around or recognizing objects. Metamorphopsia is occurring "without agnosia or imperception."[11]

Something similar can happen after taking mescaline or LSD. The subject, naturally enough, finds the experience of "change without change" difficult to put into words. But here, for example, is a woman describing what happened to her after taking LSD: "About three-quarters of an hour after the beginning of the experiment a different quality of consciousness came with a rush. Nothing was definably changed, but the room was suddenly transfigured . . . I said 'It is poignantly lovely, but I can't explain why. There is a divine ordinariness about it and yet it is completely different.'"[12]

The neuropsychologist Stephen Kosslyn has commented, in relation to metamorphopsia: "This dissociation between *experience* and function is fascinating, suggesting that the experience is produced by a collateral process . . . outside the 'chain of command' that results in recognition. If so, then this collateral path can be disrupted while the main one is left unimpaired."[13]

Kosslyn's suggestion is, I think, right on. The only reasonable inference is that sensation (which is clearly what he means here by "experience") is indeed "outside the chain of command" that leads to perceptual recognition. However, neither Kosslyn nor Weiskrantz nor others who have thought about these strange phenomena have as yet been ready to follow where, to me, they seem to obviously lead.

If sensation can be *side-lined*, then doesn't this mean that sensation is in reality some kind of *side show?* It might be going too far to suggest that sensation plays no part in perception. But I think the weight of evidence really does suggest that sensation and perception, although they are triggered by the same event, are essentially independent takes on this event, occurring not in series but

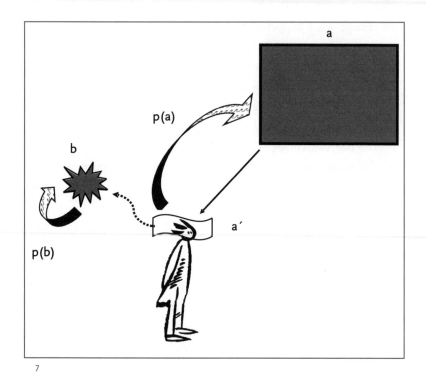

7

in parallel, and only interacting, if they ever do, much further down the line.

To cut to the chase, here is my alternative model [Figure 7].[14] The external object, a, transmits a stimulus to the sense organ, a′. The subject creates a sensation, b, as an active response to it—a *personal evaluative* response. This response is not designed to be a *copy* of the stimulus. But, just in so far as it is S's response to the particular stimulus, it carries potentially a wealth of information about the stimulus, both as to what the stimulus is as a physical event and as to how the subject feels about it. S's reading of this information, p(b), can be put to several uses (we shall come back to some of them); but the one thing it is *not* used for is as the raw material for the perception of the world. Perception has its own quite separate channel, p(a), beginning over again with the stimulus.

I have put down a series of markers here, which I shall try to explain and justify later. But, meanwhile, how about this for an analogy [Figure 8]: The mailman arrives at your house and presses the doorbell button, which rings the doorbell in the hall. The sound of the doorbell sets your dog barking in the livingroom. The barking is an evaluative response to the bell, which you can read as information both about the bell and how your dog feels about it. But you also hear the bell directly and realize the mailman is at the door!

Note that, in theory, it could be the case that you get to learn about the mailman *via* the barking dog. But let's say we can reject this possibility because we know of cases of "barklessmail," where you can guess the mailman is at the door even though the dog has been removed; and also of cases of "metamorphmail," where the dog howls instead of barking and you still read the message of the bell the same way.

!!!!

8

I will not press the analogy too far. The point is that with this scheme it is possible to see how several otherwise puzzling syndromes might result from local damage.

Figure 9 (top) would be the case of blindsight, with b and consequently p(b) destroyed but p(a) left intact. Figure 9 (middle) would

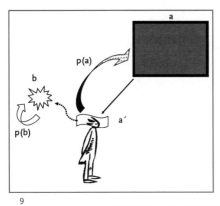

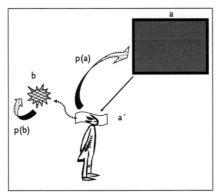

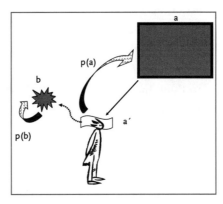

be the case of metamorphopsia, with b and consequently p(b) playing up but p(a) again intact. And Figure 9 (bottom) would be the case, not yet discussed, of visual agnosia, where p(a) has broken down but b and p(b) are still functioning normally—so that, for example, a patient can no longer name the color of an external object even though he reports there has been no loss of color sensations.[15]

And there is one other set of phenomena to which the model seems especially applicable, namely, the findings of new experiments on *sensory substitution*. Research into the possibility of substituting one kind of sensory input for another was pioneered by Paul Bach y Rita in the late 1960s.[16] Bach y Rita fitted subjects up with a device which took the image from a television camera mounted on the head and transposed it into a pattern of tactile vibration in a flat array of mechanical vibrators in contact with the skin of the trunk. He discovered that subjects wearing this device could with remarkably little practice learn to use the tactile information to make accurate visual judgments about objects in space. He called the phenomenon "skin vision," and he had no hesitation in claiming that his subjects were acquiring a limited kind of visual perception.

But what about their sensation? What kind of phenomenal experience were these subjects having? According to my model, sensation is a response to the sensory stimulus as such, and there is no reason to think that its quality—notably, its modality—will be affected by what goes on in the perceptual channel [see Figure 10]. So, even if the subject becomes capable of reading the touch stimulus a' coming

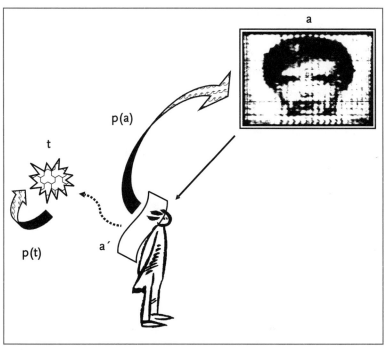

a

p(a)

t

p(t)

a'

10

from scene a as a *visual* percept p(a), he ought still to experience the sensation he is creating, t, as *tactile*, p(t).

Other theorists, however, disagree. Kevin O'Regan, Erik Myin, and Alva Nöe, for example, in a recent paper say straight out that "the quality of a sensory modality does not derive from the particular sensory input channel . . . It should therefore be possible to obtain a visual experience from auditory or tactile input."[17]

We need to know, of course, what subjects actually say. Unfortunately, Bach y Rita collected little by way of introspective reports from his subjects. In his book *Sensory Substitution,* he does note that "even during task performance . . . the subject can perceive purely tactile sensations when he is asked to concentrate on those sensations."[18] But otherwise he leaves the question of the quality of the experience hanging.

However, on this crucial issue we can turn to the more recent studies of *auditory* vision. In Chapter 2 I referred briefly to Peter Meijer's research with the vOICe apparatus. Here the TV camera transposes the picture into a "soundscape" which the subject hears through headphones [Figure 11].[19] Specifically, a visual sensor sweeps horizontally across the scene, creating a modulated sound in which brighter areas sound louder and spatially higher areas sound higher in pitch. As with the case of tactile substitution, subjects can soon become quite proficient in using this auditory device to make visual judgments.

Meijer himself poses the question: *"Is it Vision? Can it be?"*[20] It is clear that he thinks it surely *can* be. He says: "Our assumption here is that the brain is ultimately not interested in the information 'carrier' (here, sound) but only in the information 'content.'"[21] In other words, he sees no theoretical reason why auditory vision could not be

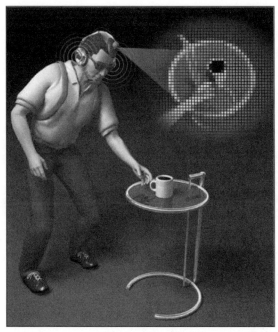

11

the qualitative equivalent of normal vision. Even so, he stops short of claiming that the evidence of his studies confirms this.

O'Regan, Myin, and Nöe, however, have no such reticence. They write: "For example, a woman wearing a visual-to-auditory substitution device will explicitly describe herself as seeing through it."[22] Well, will she really? Meijer has obtained introspective reports from his subjects, and their answers are revealingly ambivalent. One or two subjects do say straight out—though with a strong hint of bravado—that, yes, this really is like proper seeing. But more typically they report having a complicated *dual* experience—of just the kind our new model would predict. They *look* and they *hear* and they *see*.

Here are some examples of how they describe it:[23]

> I am now looking at my wife for the first time since I have gone blind. She is making a sort of squishy type of sound.

> With it, I can look at photos that people email me and with a web cam mounted on a visor I can look at my environment. Everything has its own unique sound and once you learn the principles involved you can know what you're seeing.

> Sure the soundscapes are *sound,* but it creates a different kind of input for my mind . . . There are two distinct areas of consciousness. This may seem strange, for sound to generate two different types of input for my mind. I can not explain it. I just am aware it is true.

This last subject finds it hard to explain. But if our new model is correct, then it is really not so strange for sound, as she puts it, "to generate two different types of input for my mind." As a matter of fact, light also generates two different types of input to the mind—visual sensation and perception—only we call both "seeing." And so too, though she may not have realized it, does sound in normal circumstances—auditory sensation and perception—only we call both "hearing."

I would like to be able to say we are now ready to move on. With this model of sensation and perception as independent mental processes, I think a good many puzzling phenomena fall into place. I shall be arguing, as we proceed, that with it—with this understanding of what sensation is and what it is not—we have a road map for asking the right questions about consciousness, where otherwise we might remain quite lost.

Yet I must acknowledge that, although I have been pressing this model for fifteen years now, my peers remain for the most part unpersuaded. The philosopher Daniel Dennett kindly says that "Humphrey has convinced me that something like his distinction between visual sensation and visual perception must be drawn."[24] But I cannot pretend that my support—at least among heavyweight philosophers or psychologists—extends much further.

So I want to discuss two problems for the model, which may perhaps help explain other scholars' resistance.

First is this. If sensation is *not* involved in perception, why do we *think* that it *is?* For I have to agree, we surely do think that it is—indeed, that this red sensation in front of us now, far from being a side show, *belongs to,* even *is located* at the screen. We surely do not think of it as something of *our making,* or as representing a personal interaction with light at our eyes.

Although Dennett (partly) supports me, I must acknowledge that another rank of philosophers has come down hard. Colin McGinn writes, in criticism of my position, "It is surely false to suggest that in a typical visual experience the way in which my retina is being physically stimulated is part of how things seem to me. I have no experience of my retina."[25] Robert Van Gulick protests that when he looks at a red soda can on the table, it seems to him he experiences the phenomenal color "as a feature of the can out there on the table," not as something to do with himself.[26] And Valerie Hardcastle baldly states, "We don't feel redly about parts of our visual field . . . we project our visual sensations as something external to us."[27]

Our *eyes,* these critics are objecting, are not for *seeing eyes.* No more than are noses for smelling noses. "Can you smell carrots?" says one carrot-nosed snowman to another, in the cartoon [Figure 12].[28] The cartoon makes a serious point.

I think this *is* a serious problem for my model, in fact so serious that I myself have sometimes wondered whether it may not be lethal. How can I have a theor*y* of sensations which seems obviously at odds with what people actually say they experience?

Part of the answer was given long ago by Thomas Reid. He suggested that the confusion between sensation and perception is simply an inevitable consequence of repeated association: "The perception

"Can you smell carrots?"

12

and its corresponding sensation are produced at the same time. In our experience we never find them disjoined. Hence, we are led to consider them as one thing, to give them one name, and to confound their different attributes."[29] But I would be the first to admit that this hardly seems sufficient to explain the illusion—assuming it is an illusion—that sensations belong out there where the perceived object is.

It has come to me as something of a relief, therefore, to hear of a recent discovery by the neuropsychologist V. S. Ramachandran, precisely about how sensation can be *mislocated*.[30]

In Armel and Ramachandran's experiment [Figure 13 top], a subject S sits at a table with his own hand hidden from view by a partition P, while there is a fake rubber hand FH in full view in front of him. His own real hand and the rubber hand are then tapped and stroked in synchrony by the experimenter E. What happens is that the subject reports that he feels the corresponding tactile sensations to be located *in the rubber hand.*

But here's the thing: if there is no rubber hand in view and the real hand and *a spot on the table top* are tapped and stroked in synchrony [Figure 13 bottom], the subject now says he feels the sensation to located at that *spot in the table.* What's more, if a piece of sticking plaster is placed both on the real hand and on the spot on the table, and then *the plaster on the table* is suddenly ripped off, the subject reports feeling pain and shows an emotional change in skin conductance.

This phenomenon, it must be said, was unpredicted. But, now that we know it occurs, I think it is easy to see just why we might have seen it coming. It would seem to be clearly a case of the subject's making what philosophers call an "inference to the best explanation." If a subject feels a particular pattern of tactile sensation and sees a highly correlated pattern of stroking, it will surely be perfectly rea-

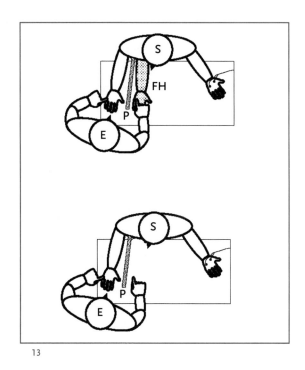

13

sonable for him to conclude *one* event rather than *two*—so that the tactile sensation must be located where the stroking is seen to be occurring.

But, now, how about the case of someone having a red sensation when he looks at a red screen? If, as S moves his eyes, he both feels a certain spatio-temporal pattern of sensation and perceives a highly correlated red-colored object in the external world, then in much the same way it will surely be reasonable and natural for him to conclude that the sensation is actually located out there in the object, where the action is.[31] This is as neat a solution as I could hope for to what might otherwise remain a major problem for my model.

Let me turn, then, to what I think is the second, very different, reason why other theorists remain unconvinced. They have a problem with what would seem to be the apparent *uselessness* of sensation. If, as I am suggesting, sensations are not involved directly in perception, then what *are* they involved in? What's *the point* of them?

I declared earlier that I myself want, in the end, to provide an evolutionary theory of why we experience the world the way we do. But, if that's the case, what am I doing proposing a model that sidelines sensations? I quoted Peter Meijer above: "Our assumption here is that the brain is ultimately not interested in the information 'carrier' but only in the information 'content.'" But if the brain—or rather the person whose brain it is—is not interested in the information carrier, which is the sensory stimulus, then why ever should the brain of this person go to the trouble of creating an exotic side show that represents the stimulus?

Well, people have evolved to have brains that *do* it. It is fair to assume the capacity has been designed-in by natural selection. So there must actually be good functional reasons for taking an interest in sensation. But what can they be?

As will be apparent later in this book, I am not against coming up with a speculative evolutionary story to explain why things have evolved to be the way they are. But, if and when it's possible, I would of course rather take the more reliable route to understanding the function of a biologically adapted system, which is to look to see what fitness-relevant failures occur when the system is disabled.

If we want to know the function of a peacock's tail, we can look to see what happens when the tail feathers are cut off. If we want to know the function of a cow's two stomachs, we can look to see what happens when the first stomach is by-passed. Likewise, in the case of sensation, we can look to see what happens in the various conditions where sensation is corrupted or eliminated.

Blindsight must surely provide an important test case. When brain damage has eliminated the capacity for visual sensation, what *functional* deficits follow? We have remarked already on what a person with blindsight *can* do, but now let's make the question what he *can't* do.

Blindsight is an unexpected and remarkable capacity. Nonetheless, we should recognize that it falls far short of normal sight in a number of crucial ways. And, interestingly enough, there seems to be a common theme to what is missing: namely that a subject who sees *without sensation* finds that in one way or another he no longer feels that his seeing has anything "to do with me." Which is, of course, just what we might expect to be the result of removing the component of experience that *is* "to do with me"—the component that is intrinsically creative and personal.

So, in the case of blindsight:[32]

• The subject does not know that he *can* do it.

To begin with, the subject typically denies that he is able to see at all in the affected part of the visual field. He has to be persuaded to guess what he is looking at, and even then he does not expect his guesses to be better than random. Not surprisingly, he does not spontaneously make use of blindsight. And, even after long practice in and confirmation of his ability, he still lacks confidence. It seems blindsight does not *belong* to him.

• The subject does not know *how* he does it.

The subject cannot explain his own ability to himself. So far as he is concerned, there is no reason why he should be able to see. It certainly does not feel to him like a case of eyesight, that's to say *vision*. Instead, he may even say that the experience has no sensory modality at all. It seems he finds blindsight *unreasonable*.

• The subject cannot *imagine* doing it.

The subject cannot picture what it's like to see in the blind field. Nor can he at all easily *remember* anything he has "blind-seen."[33] "All these subjects lack the ability to think about or to image the objects that they can respond to in another mode."[34] It seems that when the subject does not feel himself responsible in the first place, he cannot *recreate* it.

- The subject is not able to use his own experience as a basis for *attributing* the condition of seeing to someone else.

At least, I assume so. Although we would need a case of someone with nothing but blindsight from birth to confirm this, it seems obvious that, if the subject does not understand and cannot imagine it in his own case, he is not going to make use of the concept in trying to understand someone else.[35] It seems blindsight provides no basis for *empathy* or *mind-reading by simulation.*

- The subject does not *care.*

Patients with blindsight seem remarkably unexcited by their surprising abilities. They may, for example, be able to perceive color in the blind field, but they certainly never comment on its value for them. It seems blindsight—sensationless vision—is *affectless* vision.

This last point is so tantalizing and potentially significant that I am tempted to relate it to a rather different case history. I did not test my monkey Helen—as in retrospect I wish I had done—to see if she still showed the affective response to colored light that characterizes a normal monkey. But I did get highly suggestive information from a human case.[36]

H.D., a 27-year-old woman, was brought to London from Iran in 1972 to have an operation to remove cataracts from her eyes. She had been blind since the age of three. The surgeon who operated on her had promised there was a good chance of her being able to see normally again. However, when I was introduced to her, several months after the operation, I found her in a state of great despair. She was convinced the operation had been a complete failure. It seemed she could see no better than before.

There was, unfortunately, an all too probable explanation. When the visual cortex of the brain is not "exercised" by getting input from the eyes, degenerative changes are likely to occur. Since H.D.'s visual cortex had remained unused since early childhood, there was a real possibility that it was no longer able to function properly. If this were so, it meant, maybe, that H.D. was in effect in much the same condition as my monkey Helen, who had the complete visual cortex lesion. And Helen, when I first met her, was also convinced that she was blind.

But this gave me reason to look on the bright side for H.D. If her case was in some ways like Helen's, perhaps not all was lost. Perhaps, I and my colleagues thought, she would be capable of learning to see again as Helen had. (This was a couple of years before the discovery of human blindsight.)

I decided to try some of the same things with her. I took her out to "see" the sights of London. We walked the streets and parks, while I held her hand and described what was before her. And soon enough it became clear—to her as well as to me—that she did indeed have a capacity for vision of which she had not been aware. She could point to a pigeon on the square, she could reach for a flower, she could step up when she came to a curb.

After all, it seemed the operation had not been a *total* failure. H.D.'s eyes and brain were working again, at least to some degree. But was this anything like what H.D. herself was hoping for? No, in reality it only proved the more traumatic. For the awful truth, she let on, was that—just as in blindsight (and maybe it really *was* a kind of blindsight)—her vision still lacked any qualitative depth. She had been living for twenty years with the idea of how marvelous it would be if only she could see like other people. She had heard so many accounts, stories, poetry about the wonders of vision. Yet now, here she was, with part of her dream come true, and she simply *could not feel it.*

As I wrote in the scientific research report, "'Seeing', far from being a rewarding activity, had become a tiresome duty for her, and left to herself she soon lost interest in it."[37] H.D. was desperately disappointed, almost suicidal. With great courage, she finally took back control of her situation—by putting on her dark glasses again, taking up her white cane, and going back to her former status of being conventionally blind.

I realize we should not read too much into this one case. But now

I dare say of H.D., as of other cases of blindsight, that what made her vision so relatively worthless was that she did not experience it as a significant extension of her Self.

So, when sensation is absent:

• The subject thinks of him/herself as less of a Self.

Our question, a little way back, was this: If sensation is not involved directly in perception, what *is* it involved in? What is *the point* of it?

From the analysis of blindsight, a raft of answers has become apparent. What sensation does is to track the subject's *personal interaction* with the external world—creating the sense each person has of being present and engaged, lending a hereness, a nowness, a me-ness to the experience of the present moment.

This may not be all. We shall see later that the uses of sensation may go considerably further. But it is clear already that we need not worry that our model, where sensations are a side show, leaves sensations unloved and useless. Let's return to S looking at the red screen [Figure 14]. If sensation, the redding, fact b, were not a fact, if S did not bring it into being—so that he can notice it, remark on it, imagine it, take responsibility for it, attribute it, joy in it—he would be the loser.

With those problems for our model out of the way, we can now move on with some confidence to the discussion of what it means for con-

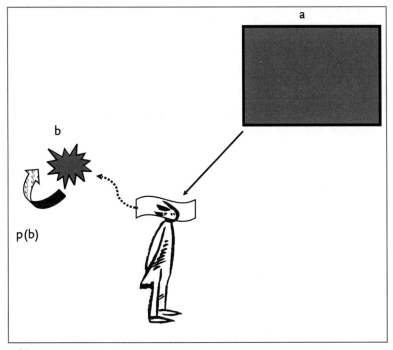

14

sciousness. Remember Fodor's remark: "Nobody has the slightest idea what consciousness is, or what it's for, or how it does what it's for (to say nothing of what it's made of)." We have not got final answers yet. But, provided we accept the starting point that it is *in having sensations* that a subject becomes *conscious,* we can claim to be making progress on two fronts. If the creation of this side show is what *having sensation is,* we have taken the first step to understanding what *consciousness is.* And if these crucial "side-effects" we have identified are some of the things *sensation is for,* we have taken the first step toward understanding what *consciousness is for.*

Of course, we must be careful not to become overconfident. We must not forget the health-warning. "Even if sensation is the vehicle and occasion of consciousness, the discovery of what conscious sensation *is* will not necessarily reveal the crucial feature of what it is that does the business." So, for example, it could be true that conscious sensation is xyz, without anything we have yet specified about xyz actually being the thing that makes it conscious.

And, by the same token, here is another warning. "The discovery of what conscious sensation is *for* will not necessarily reveal whether, let alone why, it *has to be conscious to be for this.*" So, for example, it could be true that conscious sensation plays pqr roles, without *all or any of pqr being roles it plays by virtue of being conscious.*

In fact, I should confess straight up: it seems pretty obvious that we have not yet fingered the crucial characteristic of creating a sensation that makes the subject of it conscious, nor have we demonstrated that any of the roles we have identified for sensation is a role that it plays only because the subject of it is conscious.

We have been put on notice that the key may lie with selfhood.

But it would be an understatement to say this remains to be proved. So, while I do believe we are closing in on what consciousness is and what it's for, I admit, with due deference to Fodor, that we have not yet got far with *how it does what it's for,* and still less with the big hard question of *what it's made of.* But we are on our way.

4

When the question is "What is consciousness made of?" what *kind* of answer are we looking for? We have been talking all along of conscious sensation as a *fact*. Consciousness is made of a certain kind of physical activity inside the subject's head. And this activity, we can assume, has been designed by natural selection, using nothing other than the resources of a biologically evolved nervous system.

So, does this mean the answer we want is a description at the level of *nerve cells*? This is certainly the way that much contemporary research is tending. Francis Crick and Christof Koch, for example, in a recent paper titled "A Framework for Consciousness," write: "The most difficult aspect of consciousness is the so-called 'hard problem' of qualia—the redness of red, the painfulness of pain, and so on. No one has produced any plausible explanation as to how the experience of the redness of red could arise from the actions of the brain. It appears fruitless to approach this problem head-on. Instead we are attempting to find the neural correlate(s) of consciousness (NCC), in the hope that when we can explain the NCC in causal terms, this will make the problem of qualia clearer."[1]

This idea, that what we should be looking for is the so-called neural correlate of consciousness, is coming to be widely accepted by philosophers as well as neuroscientists.[2] We should note that there are, however, potential problems with it.

To start with, we ought to be clear that what researchers usually mean by the NCC is really the NBC—the neural *basis* of consciousness, the sufficient and quite likely necessary events in the brain. As Crick and Koch go on to say: "In round terms, the NCC is the minimal set of neuronal events that gives rise to a specific aspect of a conscious percept."

There is meant to be, in short, an *identity* between consciousness and the NCC. Thus, in the case of conscious sensation (Crick and Koch refer to a conscious "percept," but let's assume it is really sensation that's at issue), we can express it in terms of an equation, where the "equals" sign means "refers to the same fact in the world as":

experience of sensation = neuronal activity

However, for two facts to be the *same* fact has to mean more than that they are correlated. Identity implies necessity, correlation only contingency. We do not say, for example, that Lincoln was merely the "human correlate of the President of the United States."

But there is another reason why the NCC may not be quite the thing we need to explain consciousness. This is that the concept of the neural correlate privileges neuronal events over all the other ways we might wish to describe what is going on in the brain. One of the real (if rare) achievements of recent philosophy of mind has been the promotion of a new way of understanding mind-body equations, namely, functionalism. The basic premise of functionalism is that what really counts toward making a mental state the state it is is not so much the particular physical events that underpin it as the way in which these events play at a computational level—not the particular hardware but the logical operations that are being performed. In which case we should be looking for the FCC, the functional correlate of consciousness, rather than the NCC.

Still, maybe these are quibbles. Broadly speaking, should we regard the Crick and Koch project as a good one?

Let's go back to the example of seeing the red screen [Figure 14]. We made a case in the previous chapter for believing that the experience of having a red sensation amounts at a functional level to *doing* something, doing the business that we call redding: *experience of red = neuronal activity b = redding.*

If and when neuroscientists are able to describe what is happening—synapse by synapse, or logic gate by logic gate—from the moment the red light enters the subject's eyes to his creating and commenting on the neuronal activity, *will* it, as Crick and Koch suggest, "make the problem of qualia clearer"? Will it make it clearer why the experience is like what it is?

Yes, I am afraid it will make the *problem* horribly clearer! It will make it clear just how far we are from understanding *how any such identity could possibly be true*. For it will now seem all too obvious what is wrong with the equation: namely, that the *dimensions* of the terms on each side of the equation do not match up.[3]

I use the term "dimensions" with a particular intent. When we do physics at school we are taught that the "physical dimensions" of each side of an equation must be the same. If one side has the dimensions of a volume, the other side must be a volume too and it cannot be an acceleration; if one side has the dimensions of power, the other side must be power too and it cannot be momentum; and so on. As A. S. Ramsey put this in his classical *Dynamics* textbook: "The consideration of dimensions is a useful check in dynamical work, for each side of an equation must represent the same physical thing and therefore must be of the same dimensions in mass, space and time."[4] Indeed, so strong a constraint is this that, as Ramsey goes on, "sometimes a consideration of dimensions alone is sufficient to determine the form of the answer to a problem"—to determine the right form and equally the wrong form.

But if this is true of physical equations, it is surely no less true of all other types of identity equations. The only identities that can possibly be valid are those where both sides have the same *conceptual* dimensions, represent the same *kind* of thing. Proverbially, if we have apples on one side, we must have apples, not oranges, on the other.

So, for example, the equation $e = mc^2$ can work as an identity because—but only because—energy does have the dimensions of mass times velocity squared; $e = mc^3$, on the other hand, obviously cannot work. The equation *one hundred pence = one pound* can work because both sides are sums of money; *one hundred pence = one month* cannot.

Now, by the same token, we must face the fact that the equation *experience of red = redding* will work only provided the experience and the redding can be seen to be conceptually equivalent. But the problem is that the way people have typically talked about the phenomenology of sensation, on one side, and the NCC or whatever on the other, does not even begin to get these two terms into the same conceptual ballpark. As the philosopher Colin McGinn has colorfully put it: "Isn't it perfectly evident to you that . . . [the brain] is just the wrong kind of thing to give birth to [phenomenal] consciousness. You might as well assert that numbers emerge from biscuits or ethics from rhubarb."[5]

You will have realized no doubt that, in taking the new line I have about sensation, I have been preparing the ground for an attempt to bring the two sides closer together. But I can hardly pretend that we are there yet.

It is time, therefore, to get much more specific. We need to take a closer look at just what kind of thing sensation is—looking for ways to open it out, redescribe it, so as to make a bridge to the kind of thing that could plausibly be going on in a biologically-evolved brain.

So, let's ask again: What is having a sensation *like?* What is "what it's like to be having a sensation" *like?* And let's hope that, in trying to find the thing that it is like, we shall do better than the philosopher Natika Newton has suggested that we shall. "Phenomenal consciousness," she writes in a recent paper, "itself is *sui generis*. Nothing else is like it *in any way at all*" (Newton's italics).[6] If she were right in this, we might as well give up at once. I am happy to tell you I do not think she is right. And yet I will not deny that, unless things go well for us, she could be right.

The difficulty is the one that has haunted our discussion of sensation from early on—the difficulty of pinning down that elusive extra ingredient, the X factor. We have several times had occasion to stress that when, for example, S has the experience of redding, S—even as the subject of it—does not entirely know what "what it's like" is like, or at any rate he certainly cannot *say.* The limited reading S can make—the propositional paraphrase—is by no means the full story. Therefore, the real danger remains that in looking for the kind of thing the experience is like, we shall succeed in finding something that is like it in all but the one crucial respect the subject cannot describe.

In which case our strategy is clear. We must do the best we can do. We must try to characterize what kind of thing sensation is on the basis of those properties we *can* describe. Then, if and when we succeed in finding a comparable kind of thing on the brain side of the equation, perhaps—just perhaps—this will turn out to hold the key to the further properties we *cannot* describe. Perhaps the effable will deliver the ineffable.

I have hinted heavily already how I think our analysis should go. When, for example, S looks at the red screen, he *creates* the sensation, he experiences it in the creation, and then he gets a partial glimpse of what's going on. So, presumably the place we should be looking for analogies for this *kind* of thing is with other things that S, as the subject, creates, experiences in the creation, and has (limited) access to.

I believe there is one category, and one only, that fills the bill. We named it early on in Chapter 2. It is the category of *actions*—the things S does with the one part of the universe over which he as a subject has direct control, his own *body*. But, to localize it further, I believe the analogy is even closer to a subclass of bodily actions, namely *expressions*—the things S does with his body specifically to show how he feels about what is immediately happening to him—a smile, a shout, a tear, a shake of the fist.

I have made the detailed case for this in an earlier book.[7] Here, let's be content to see how the analogy plays out in relation to five defining characteristics of the experience of sensation. We can take the example of a person creating a red sensation at his eyes or a pain in his toe, on the experience side, and compare it with the example of his creating a smile with his lips, on the expression side.

Ownership. Sensations always belong to the subject. When S experiences the red sensation, or equally when he experiences the pain, S *owns* the sensation, it is his and no one else's, S is the one and only *author* of it. As, when S smiles, he owns and is the author of this expression.

Bodily location. Sensations are always indexical and invoke a particular part of the subject's body. S feels the red sensation in *this* part of his visual field, S feels the pain in *this* part of his foot. As, when S smiles with his lips, the smiling intrinsically involves this part of his face.

Presentness. Sensations are always present tense, ongoing and imperfect. When S experiences the red sensation or feels the pain, the sensation is here just *now for the time being.* The experience did not exist before, and will not exist after S stops feeling it. As, when S smiles, the smiling too exists just now.

Qualitative modality. Sensations always have the feel of one of several qualitatively distinct modalities. When S has the red sensation, it belongs to the class of *visual* sensations; but when he has the pain, it belongs to the wholly different class of *somatic* sensations. Each modality, linked to its own class of sense organ, has, as it were, its own distinct phenomenal style. As, when S smiles with his lips, this expression belongs to the class of *facial expressions,* as contrasted with, say, vocal expressions or lachrymatory ones. Each expressive modality, linked to its own class of effector organ, has its own distinct medium and style of expression.

Phenomenal immediacy. Most important, sensation for the subject is always phenomenally immediate, and the four properties just described are self-disclosing. Thus, when S has the red sensation, his impression is simply that "I'm redding, now, in this part of my visual field of my eyes"—and the fact that it's S's eyes (rather than someone else's), that it's this place in his *eyes* (rather than some other place in him), that it's happening *now* (rather than some other time), and that it's something occurring in a *visual* way (rather than, say, in an auditory or olfactory way) are facts of which S is directly and immediately aware for the very reason that it is S, the author of the red sensation, who makes these facts. So, too, when S smiles with his lips, his impression is simply that his lips are smiling, and all the corresponding properties of this action are facts of which he, the author of the smile, is immediately aware for similar reasons.

In these five ways, and others we could point to, the positive analogies add up. Admittedly, there is no sign yet that we have cornered the X factor. We certainly cannot yet claim that bodily expressions, as such, have any of that special "what it's like" richness. But we knew we might not get everything at once.

Let's see what we *have* got. If we look again at the problematical identity equation, *experience of red sensation = redding,* is the task of matching the dimensions of conscious sensation on the left and redding on the right looking any easier? Well, perhaps, yes. As Ramsey wrote, "Sometimes a consideration of dimensions alone is going to be sufficient to determine the form of the answer to a problem." If sensation is indeed like a kind of bodily expression, then the activity of redding must also be like a kind of bodily expression. And this, after all is not *such* a tall order. Indeed, if the redding is *like* a kind of bodily expression, why should it not actually *be* a kind of bodily expression?

This would be, of course, a neat solution. But is it a solution for which we could possibly provide independent arguments? In the previous chapter we established a picture of sensation as a personal evaluative response to stimulation occurring at the body surface that "carries potentially a wealth of information about the stimulus, both as to what the stimulus is as a physical event and as to how the subject feels about it." This certainly holds promise. Is there now a further story we can tell to link sensory response to bodily expression?

There is. Since the start of this inquiry we have been coupling the questions "What is consciousness?" and "How did it evolve?" Now I would suggest that it is only by taking an evolutionary perspective that we can begin to see what this is all about.

So, let me tell a story about the evolution of sensation, feeling, and perception—a story that begins with a primitive amoeba and ends with human beings. It will not be a story you should take too literally. Indeed, it will correspond only loosely to the historical reality. But that's all right. What we need at this stage of the argument is a heuristic to guide our thinking. And for this it will be sufficient if we can reconstruct a *possible* evolutionary trajectory—a route by which our ancestors *might* have got from there to here.[8]

Take a deep breath.

Let us return in imagination to the earliest of times and envision a primitive amoebalike animal floating in the ancient seas. This animal has a defining edge to it, a structural boundary. The boundary is crucial. The animal exists within the boundary—everything inside it is part of "self," everything outside is part of "other." The boundary is the vital frontier across which exchanges of material and energy and information can take place.

Now light falls on the animal, objects bump into it, pressure waves press against it, chemicals stick to it. No doubt some of these surface events are going to be a good thing for the animal, others bad. If it is to survive, it must evolve the ability to sort out the good from the bad and to respond differently—reacting to this stimulus with an ouch! to that with a whoopee!

At the beginning, these wriggles are entirely local responses, organized immediately around the site of stimulation [Figure 15 top]. But later there develops something more like a reflex arc, passing via a central ganglion or protobrain [Figure 15 bottom]. What's more, there begin to be specialized sensory areas: this area specialized for sensing chemicals, that one for light, and so on.

15

Thus, when, say, salt arrives at its skin, the animal detects it and makes a characteristic wriggle of activity—it wriggles "saltily." When red light falls on it, it makes a different kind of wriggle—it wriggles "redly." Such behavior has evolved to be biologically appropriate, with each response being nicely adapted to where and how the body is being stimulated.

These responses are the prototypes of later "sensation," as we humans know it [compare Figure 7:b]. Still, as yet, in the primitive animal these sensory responses are nothing other than responses—mere wriggles of acceptance or rejection. There is no reason to suppose the animal is in any way mentally aware of what is happening on any level.

We can imagine, however, that as this animal's life becomes more complex, the time comes when it will indeed be advantageous for it to have some kind of inner knowledge of what is affecting it, which it can begin to use as a basis for more sophisticated planning and decision making. It needs the capacity to form a *mental representation* of the stimulation at the surface of its body.

Now, one way of developing this capacity might be to start over again with a completely fresh analysis of the incoming information from the sense organs. But this would be to miss a trick. For the fact is that all the requisite details about the stimulation—where the stimulus is occurring, what kind of stimulus it is, and how it should be dealt with—are already encoded in the *command signals* the animal is issuing when it makes the appropriate sensory response. Thus, the way is open for the animal to discover what is happening and even how it feels about it by the simple trick of *monitoring what it itself is doing about it.*

Imagine, by analogy, how you might be able to tell what someone is hearing on the telephone simply by listening to what she is saying

16

in reply, or even by observing the look on her face [Figure 16]. Jean Cocteau made a whole play, *La voix humaine,* out of a woman's one-sided telephone conversation with her ex-lover—the content of the other side being entirely transparent to the audience from her responses.

Imagine, better still, how you might be able to tell what she is watching on an audio-video link. She is receiving calls from different countries, informing her about the local scene [Figure 17]. You can tell from her language, her tone, and the words she uses where the

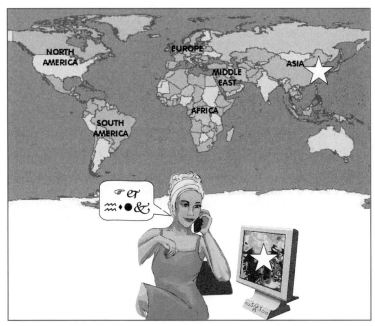

17

call is coming from and what it means to her. Now she's talking Yankee, now Japanese, now she's laughing, now crying into the receiver.

So imagine, still further, how, if you were her, you might be able to tell *what you yourself are watching and hearing* by *monitoring your own replies.* Then perhaps it is in just such a way, that our animal ancestors, in reality, begin to keep track mentally of what is happening at their body surface by attending to their own responses. Thus, for example, to sense the presence of salt at a certain location, the animal monitors its own command signals for wriggling saltily at that location, or, to sense the presence of red light, it monitors its signals for wriggling redly [Figure 18]. This does not tell it all there is, but it tells it all that, at this stage, it needs to know.

Here is a different analogy. You are sitting at a cinema organ, watching the movie that is being projected on the screen, and as the scenes change you make music to match the mood and content of what you see going on. Now, the way you represent to yourself what the movie is about is by listening to the very music you are creating!

This self-monitoring by the subject of his own response is the prototype of "feeling sensation," as we humans know it [compare Figure 7:p(b)].

We should note that up until this stage of evolution the animal's concerns have remained entirely local. By monitoring its own responses, the animal forms a representation of the stimulation arriving at its own body surface. But, so far, it neither knows nor cares where the stimuli are coming from, let alone what they may imply about the world beyond its body.

Yet would the animal not be better off if it *were* to care about the world beyond? Let's say a pressure wave presses against its side—would it not be better off if it were able to interpret this stimulus as signaling an approaching predator? A chemical odor drifts across its

18

skin—would it not be better off if it were able to interpret this as signaling the presence of a tasty worm?

The answer of course is yes. And we can be sure that soon enough our ancestors do in fact hit on the idea of using the information contained in body surface stimulation for this novel purpose. However, when it comes to it, this purpose turns out to be *so* novel that a very different style of information-processing is needed. When the question is "What is happening locally to me?" the answer that is wanted is qualitative, present-tense, transient, and subjective. When the question is "What is happening out there in the world?" the answer that is wanted is quantitative, analytical, permanent, and objective.

So, to cut a long story short, the solution is to develop a separate processing channel independent of the primitive one, a channel that this time really does start over with a fresh analysis of information coming from the sense organs. While the old channel continues to provide an affect-laden modality-specific body-centered picture of what the stimulation is doing to the animal's own self, the second is set up to provide a more neutral, abstract, body-independent representation of the outside world [Figure 19]. This second channel is—of course—the prototype of perception as we humans know it [compare Figure 7:p(a)].

Now, we may assume that from this point on, sensation and perception continue along relatively independent paths in evolution. But we can ignore for now what happens to perception, because it is the fate of sensation that interests us.

At the stage we left it, the animal is still actively responding to stimulation with overt bodily activity, and these sensory responses continue to be biologically adaptive. Yet, as this animal continues to evolve and becomes more independent of its immediate environment, it will presumably have less and less to gain from continuing to respond directly to the surface stimuli as such.

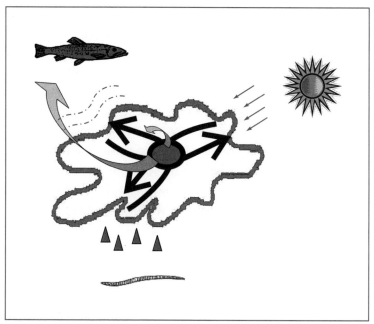

19

Then why not simply give up on this primitive kind of local responding altogether? The reason why not will surely be that, even though the animal may no longer have anything to gain from responding to stimuli directly, it still wants to be able to keep apprised of, and up to date on, what's happening to its own body. The external world is the external world, and it is certainly useful to know what is going on out there. But let the animal never forget that the bottom line is its own bodily well-being, that *I am nobody if I'm not me*. And since the way it has been learning about "what is happening to *me*" has been by monitoring the command signals for its own responses, it clearly cannot afford to stop making these responses altogether.

Thus, the animal must at the very least continue to issue commands such as *would* produce an appropriate response at the right place on the body *if* they were to carry through into bodily behavior. However, given that the overt behavior is no longer wanted, it will be better now if these commands remain *virtual* or *as-if* commands—commands that, while retaining their original intentional and indexical properties, do not in fact have any real effects.

The upshot is—or so I have argued in my earlier writings—that, over evolutionary time, there is a slow but remarkable change. What happens is that the whole sensory activity gets "privatized": the command signals for sensory responses get short-circuited before they reach the body surface, so that instead of reaching all the way out to the peripheral site of stimulation they now reach only to points more and more central on the incoming sensory pathways, until eventually the whole process becomes closed off from the outside world in an internal loop within the brain [Figure 20].

The as-if sensory responses, which are now addressed to an as-if bodily map, have lost all their original biological importance and have in fact disappeared from view. But this privacy has come about only relatively late in evolution (perhaps not being completed, in the line that led to humans, until the evolution of the mammalian cere-

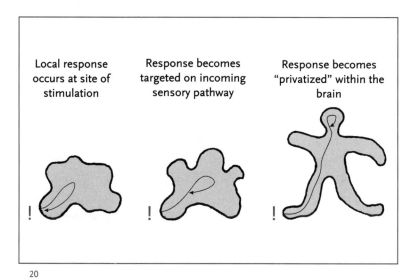

Local response occurs at site of stimulation

Response becomes targeted on incoming sensory pathway

Response becomes "privatized" within the brain

20

bral cortex). And by this time there is every reason to suppose that the forms of the responses and the quality of the sensations that correspond to them will have been more or less permanently fixed. So we might expect later generations to continue to experience body surface stimulation, even today, in a way which reflects this evolutionary pedigree. That's to say, sensations, which started their evolutionary life as dedicated wriggles of acceptance or rejection in response to particular forms and qualities of stimulation, will still be recognizably of their kind right down to the present day.

Let us bring this up to date. Come with me to the southwest of Ireland, where a primitive tetrapod crawled out of the sea 365 mil-

21

lion years ago and left tracks in the mud. Here I am with my family looking at the footprints [Figure 21].[9] Now here is our friend S, in the garden of my cottage close by [Figure 22]. He is taking in the stimuli at his eyes, ears, skin. S *feels* the waves of his ancient sensory responses, while at the same time, separately, he *perceives* the lake, the sky, the trees.

22

You know Yeats's poem, *The Lake Isle of Innisfree:* "I hear lake water lapping with low sounds by the shore," "there midnight's all a glimmer, and noon a purple glow, and evening full of the linnet's wings," "I'll live alone in the bee-loud glade." Here S is, in this multisensory environment [Figure 23]. And here is the organist inside him, playing to the ever-changing picture, while the complex many-stranded lines of music create those vibrations in his soul.

It is time to take stock. Suppose the evolutionary story I have sketched is something like right. What does it buy us, in terms of sci-

23

entific understanding? I would say that, to put it at its least, it allows us to see how the mind-brain identity equation for sensations *could* work.

Let me recap. For the mind side of the equation, our earlier analysis suggested that the experience of creating a sensation has many of the characteristics of creating a bodily expression. Now, for the brain side, we have constructed a history which suggests that sensations are the descendants of a kind of activity which once upon a time actually *was* a kind of bodily expression. True, the activity on the brain side nowadays is virtual, privatized, addressed to an as-if body; but there is every reason to suppose that its characteristics—its dimensions—have remained in line with what they were.

I must admit that, in seeing how this could work, we are not yet seeing much more than the working of the very features we have artfully built into our theory of it. We knew we needed on both sides of the equation the hereness, nowness, and me-ness of sensory experience. We needed the affective dimension, the immediacy coupled with limited accessibility.

It is satisfying—and just as well—that we have been able to find all of these features we needed, coming together in the context of a reasonably plausible historical account. But since the beginning of this chapter, we have been trading on the hope that with luck we would get *more* than we built in: especially that what we uncovered on the brain side of the equation would help us make sense of our inchoate intuition that there is something quite *else* on the mind side.

Are we any closer to netting that elusive X factor? If we are, I confess it is as yet far from obvious. But the theory is young, and other things are going our way. In fact, there is one other thing that is going our way, quite unexpectedly—a promising new feature emerging from the evolutionary account that we did not build in. This feature, as we shall see, is of such significance in its own right that it will pay us to break the narrative in order to discuss it.

5

The development that we did not anticipate is this. By putting sensation within the sphere of agency, on the *production* side of the mind rather than the *reception* side, what we get from our model of sensation is the possibility of a significant degree of *central control of what it's like.*

Let's go back to the analogy of someone monitoring her own responses to an incoming telephone call [Figure 16]. We imagined how the subject might represent the incoming message by attending to what she herself is saying in reply. But we might have seen a further possibility. For while the subject probably has little if any control over the incoming message as such, quite possibly she will have considerable control over her own vocal response. And this must mean that her representation of the incoming call is something that in a surprising way *depends on her.*

For example, suppose she were to be able to modulate the emotional quality of her voice—speaking more loudly or more softly or changing the timbre, according to her mood. In that case, just because it is her own voice that she is monitoring, she will find herself representing the same incoming message differently at different times. Depression or elation could affect the outcome, as could psychogenic drugs, alcohol, cannabis, or LSD.

But still more dramatic possibilities may open up. For, besides being able to control the quality of her response to the input, she may be able to suppress her response altogether or to *invent* it. That's to say, it may be within her power to speak as if in answer to a caller without any input at all.

I mentioned in the previous chapter Jean Cocteau's play *La voix humaine.* In the play the actress on stage conducts a highly charged telephone conversation with her lover, while we in the audience can guess what he is saying from her words. But actually there is nothing her lover is saying. This is a one-woman play in which the actress is actually getting no cue from the telephone receiver. But just imagine, now, that she were to be monitoring her own speech as evidence of what she is supposedly hearing: she would in effect be *hallucinating* the existence of her lover at the end of the line!

If the analogy holds, it would have clear and exciting implications for the real-life experience of sensation. We could now see why, according to our model, sensation should be especially amenable to top-down influences, probably much more than perception of the external world is.

To start with, we might expect to find sensation itself being affected by changes in mood or by mind-altering drugs. And remember we saw in Chapter 3 how psychogenic drugs such as mescaline and LSD can in fact alter the quality of sensory experience (while leaving perception relatively unaffected). Endogenous mood changes, such as depression, are reported to do so also.

Furthermore, we might expect to find sensation sometimes being entirely self-generated. So sensation could be at the center of vivid imagery, as in visions or dreams. While relatively few people may have experienced waking hallucinations, each of us knows the phenomenal richness of the sensations we seem able to manufacture in our dreams.

And, more still, we might expect to find sensation playing a key role in people's ability to *simulate* the mental states of other people. Indeed, sensation as bodily expression would seem tailor-made for *projective empathy.*

Let's return to the introductory discussion of Chapter 2. We drew attention to the issue of co-consciousness. We remarked how, when people are in each other's presence, they instinctively make bridges into each other's minds. Our subject, S, sees *you* seeing red [Figure 3].

Friedrich Nietzsche (though he is seldom given credit for it) was one of the first to emphasize this fundamental social dimension of consciousness. "Consciousness," he wrote, "is really only a net of communication between human beings; it is only as such that it had to develop; a solitary human being who lived like a beast of prey would not have needed it."[1]

But Nietzsche was one of the first to provide an explanation of how the net is made.

> To understand another person, that is to imitate his feelings in ourselves, we . . . produce the feeling in ourselves by imitating with our own body the expression of his eyes, his voice, his walk, his bearing. Then a similar feeling arises in us in consequence of an ancient association between movement and sensation. We have brought our skill in understanding the feelings of others to a high state of perfection and in the presence of another person we are always almost involuntarily practicing this skill.[2]

The idea that empathy is mediated by *imitating bodily action* was in the 1880s remarkably prescient. But in recent years many psychologists have come around to it, on both theoretical and empirical grounds. Stephanie Preston and Frans de Waal, for example, argued in 2002 for what they call a "perception action model" as a general explanation of empathy.[3]

Yet we still need to understand the cognitive/neurophysiological mechanism. Nietzsche writes in the passage above of "an ancient association between movement and sensation." He presumably does not mean by this quite the sort of association we have been discussing. He is referring, rather, to the fact that certain emotions follow on from movements as a secondary consequence, because the subject instinctively evaluates his own movements in this way. Frown and you'll find yourself feeling angry, smile and you'll find yourself feeling happy. So, Nietzsche is suggesting, *imitate* someone else's frown or their smile and you'll find yourself sharing their anger or their happiness.

This is the thrust of Preston and de Waal's argument as well. But suppose, in line with our new understanding of how sensations work, that sensations at the most basic level—sensations of pain, smell, color—actually *are* a kind of covert movement. Then the way could be open for imitation of action to have a much wider role in mediating empathy across the board. Not just empathy for moods and emotions, but empathy for purer sensory experiences, too. Imitate someone else's *doing the redding* and you'll find yourself sharing their experience of a red sensation.

What's more, this suggests a whole new role for the recently discovered phenomenon of "mirror neurons." These are a type of neuron in the pre-motor cortex of the brain with a remarkable dual role: they become active both when the subject performs a particular action—grasping a nut by the fingers, for example—*and* when he sees another individual doing the very same thing. Such neurons effectively link the *observation of action by someone else* to the *execution of action by oneself.* They were first described in the brains of monkeys and have now been shown to exist in the human brain as well.[4]

But if sensations are a kind of action, then the possibility arises that there may be "sensory mirror neurons," in other words neurons that link the *observation of someone else having a sensation* to the *execution of a similar sensation oneself.* And indeed there is tantalizing new evidence that there are neurons in the human brain that do in fact have mirror properties for pain. Bill Hutchison has described neurons in the anterior cingulate cortex that respond both when a human subject receives a painful stimulus such as a pinprick and also when the subject observes someone else receiving a pinprick.[5]

Can this really be what it seems? At first we might well question how it can be. The subject cannot actually be observing the other person creating a pain sensation, because the sensory response as such is private. So what exactly can a mirror neuron for pain be mirroring?

There is a particular finding in monkeys that arguably holds the key. This is that certain mirror neurons respond not only when the monkey observes another individual performing a complete action but also when the monkey observes the action *being completed out of sight*—a nut being grasped just behind a barrier, for example. The suggestion is that the neuron imitates the action the monkey *expects* is taking place.

Suppose now, in the case of pain, when the subject sees someone else receiving a pinprick, he expects that a pain sensation is likewise being created out of sight. Then a pain mirror neuron could indeed imitate this private event. If it happens this way for pain, then presumably it could happen this way for other sensory modalities as well.[6]

In our enthusiasm for this explanation, we should be careful, however, not to run ahead of the phenomena. We ought to ask: how like the *real thing* is empathetic sensation? Does the pain felt by an observer of someone else's pain really *hurt?* The answer seems to be that, for most people, the reflected sensation does not have the full intensity of sensation elicited directly.

The great economist, Adam Smith, discussed the example of how a person might typically respond to the sight of another person being tortured or beaten:

> By the imagination we place ourselves in his situation, . . . and thence
> form some idea of his sensations, and even feel something which,
> though weaker in degree, is not altogether unlike them . . . When we
> see a stroke aimed and just ready to fall upon the leg or arm of an-
> other person, we naturally shrink and draw back our own leg or our
> own arm; and when it does fall, we feel it in some measure, and are
> hurt by it as well as the sufferer.[7]

As a rule I think it's fair to say that mirrored sensory responses—if indeed this is what lies behind it—seem to be a somewhat attenuated version of normal sensory responses (just as, in fact, mirrored bodily movements are). However it is worth noting the existence of certain exceptional cases where the empathetic response is at full strength. Here, for example, is a case report of a man, who, while being hypersensitive to pain in general, appears to have felt his wife's pain as if it were quite the equal of his own:

> He was reported to be very sensitive to touch; even the slightest hand contact gave the impression of sharp fingernails. Of particular interest was his widow's recent observation that "If I slightly knocked my finger, spontaneously showing him, he would immediately grasp his own finger and say 'don't do that' [meaning not to show him]; He actually felt it. If I merely commented [that I had knocked my finger], there was no such reaction." In interview, she recounted other similar events. The experience was suddenly immediate and intense, and, apparently, qualitatively similar to the hypersensitivity occasioned by actual contact.[8]

The essayist Michel de Montaigne was another in whom empathy was nearly on a level with direct experience: "Everyone feels its impact, but some are knocked over by it. On me it makes such an intense impression, my practice is rather to avoid it than to resist it . . . the sight of another's anguish gives me real pain, and my body has often taken over the sensations of some person I am with. A persistent cougher tickles my lungs and my throat."[9]

Susanne Langer has written of the "involuntary breach of individual separateness" that takes place when a person reflexively feels himself to be in another person's place.[10] No doubt the extent of the projection varies from one person to another. Yet, few if any either can or do avoid it. Thus, human beings are indeed involuntarily caught in Nietzsche's net of shared experience—the net that is a crucial feature, perhaps *the* crucial feature, of human social life.

I think we can claim it as a major strength of our model of sensation that it provides new insight into why this involuntary breach of separateness occurs.[11] In fact if we were to revisit the evolutionary story, I suggest we might want to count empathetic mirroring as an important way in which sensation, as a form of covert bodily expression, continues to play a significant role in the biological survival of humans—and presumably other social mammals, too.

6

We now have in hand most of the features of sensation that we were looking for—with sensation as a basis for empathy coming as an unexpected bonus. With the theory shaping up so well, do we dare at last address the *hard* problem, the X factor?

It has been our stated hope that, with luck, what we uncovered on the brain side of the identity equation might help us see just why and how a suitably marvelous extra feature could emerge on the sensation side. As things are, it seems this has not happened yet. "Fallen into our lap" the X factor has not.

But can we be sure we would recognize it if it *had?* "The truth," wrote Robert Pirsig, "knocks at the door, and you say 'Go away, I'm looking for the truth,' and so it goes away."[1] While we still have so little idea of just what we are looking for—with nothing but half-formed wordless intuitions to guide us—is it likely we shall see the potential relevance of what we have uncovered, even if it is precisely what we need?

Lest we are in fact missing something obvious, let's have one last go at capturing what people's intuitions about the X factor are. What have other philosopher-psychologists been *trying* to say about what we cannot say?

It is not that other theorists have not tried. Some brave souls have tried and tried again, even if most have given up. It has become a cliché among a certain class of critic (Sutherland, Fodor, and others) to disparage their achievements. Yet, if we look more closely and kindly at the recent literature, we may see that, despite the disputes and recurrent disillusionment, the picture that is emerging is not all dark. There is even beginning to be a measure of consensus, at least about where the X-ity of the X factor is coming from.

If this X factor has to do with anything, it has to do with *time*. Consciousness has a paradoxical dimension of temporal "depth." The present moment, the "now" of sensations, is experienced as "temporally thick." Here is how Natika Newton has put it in a recent paper: "Because our present experience includes (at least) two distinct times, it is experienced not as an instantaneous slice of time but as an extended time, containing elements of both 'now' and 'not-now,' in a unified immediate representation."[2] Or, here is how I put it myself, a decade earlier:

Suppose the present were to be stretched-out a bit. Suppose it were to last long enough for the present and the past to overlap. Suppose that, in T. S. Eliot's words:

> Time present and time past
> Were both perhaps present in time future,
> And time future contained in time past.

Suppose indeed that human beings travel through life as in a "time ship," that like a spaceship has a prow and a stern and *room inside* for us to move around.

Well, in that case we would not be talking about the "present" as a physicist defines it. We might, however, be talking about the "subjective present" as we actually experience it. The "physical present," strictly speaking, is a mathematical abstraction of infinitely short duration, and nothing happens in it. By contrast the "subjective present" is arguably the carrier and *container* of our conscious life, and everything that ever happens to us happens *in it*.[3]

I called this extended present the "thick moment of consciousness." However, I did not see what Natika Newton has gone on to see: that this temporal thickness may be not only part of the answer but also part of the problem. Her interesting new idea is that the reason we are unable to get our minds around the special quality of consciousness, let alone express it in words, is precisely because the notion of the "extended present" is, by commonsense standards, *incoherent.* The very nature of the X factor makes it "analytically, ostensively and comparatively indefinable."[4]

As the mathematician Frank Ramsey (son of A. S. Ramsey, author of my *Dynamics* textbook) memorably quipped: "What we can't say we can't say, and we can't whistle it either."[5]

But wait. Could this be where our philosophers have got it, tactically, plumb wrong? Is it really so obvious we can't whistle it? Maybe we can. Maybe there are in fact *nonverbal* ways of getting at the nature of phenomenal experience that we can turn to—if not for the full scientific answer, at least for a fresh perspective or new metaphors.

A poem, as Helen Vendler said in the passage I quoted earlier, is much more than its propositional content. And the same might be said to be true of painting, music, and other arts as well. In fact, the nineteenth-century philosopher Henry Sidgwick argued that the essential quality of a work of art always transcends description: "However subtly we state in general terms the objective relations of elements in a delightful work of art, on which its delight seems to depend, we must always feel that it would be possible to produce out of similar elements a work corresponding to our general description which would give no delight at all."[6]

What's it like to be a painting? What a question. The answer has to be: probably not much. But the point of asking such a question is to prompt the thought that perhaps certain works of art do have the property of being in a special way "like something," a something that again is very hard to capture in words.

Allow me a minute to play with just this thought. Suppose there is an analogy between a work of art and "a work of sensation," where can we go with it? Well, to start with, we might want to use artistic methods and media instead of ordinary language as analytic tools for exploring the nature of phenomenal experience. Which is what certain artists have quite deliberately done.

Among contemporary artists, no one has taken this mission more seriously than the painter Bridget Riley. Riley might be called the great priestess of sensation—an artist who explicitly acknowledges the "dual province of the senses," making central to her vision the distinction between sensation and perception that we discussed in Chapter 2. Riley is not interested in representing the outside world as she *perceives* it, as an impersonal fact. She wants only to show how it *affects her*—her eyes, her body:

> If I am outside in nature, I do not look for something or at things. I try to absorb sensations without censoring them, without identifying them. I want them to come through the pores of my eyes, as it were— on a particular level of their own . . . I try to take sensation and build, with the relationships it demands, a plastic fabric which has no other *raison d'être* except to accommodate the sensation it solicits.[7]

She is struggling to find the words, and not entirely succeeding. But we have her paintings as such to help us get her meaning. And if

I may tell you my interpretation, having looked and listened and looked again, it is this. What Riley is trying to say, and what she expresses so much more effectively in the painting itself, is the idea that the key to sensation being "like something" does in fact lie in *the experience being like itself in time.*

"Feel the light," she says to an interviewer, sitting at a café table. "No, don't think about it, don't think about what's out there, just feel this moment at your eye." And the painting she creates to represent the moment—a painting of repetitive flat colored diamonds—is full of *self-similarity,* of *rhyme.* In a strange way, the painting, like the moment, is *about itself.*

Riley is known as an abstract impressionist. And she comes of course from a tradition. A century before her, the founder of natural impressionism, Claude Monet, took the lead in tackling the same semiphilosophical issues. With a very different technique, using a thick brush and layered paint and returning to the same subject matter in canvas after canvas, Monet set out almost obsessively to capture the peculiar quality of present-tense experience.

Monet wrote in a letter in 1891: "I am working very hard, struggling with a series of different effects . . . the more I continue, the more I see that a great deal of work is necessary in order to succeed in rendering what I seek; 'instantaneity.'"[8]

As Joachim Pissarro describes it, discussing Monet's series of paintings of Rouen Cathedral:

Monet not only completely banished any narrative intention from his series, he reduced each painting to the representation of one particular slice of time—to the exclusion of what happened before or after . . . Each painting is the immediate vision of an "effect" that took place "instantaneously" on the cathedral facade, in front of Monet's eyes. It may not be sheer coincidence that almost every painting of the cathedral centres on the clock: a clock that, ironically a victim of the vicissitudes of time, eventually fell off the wall and is no longer visible. The "before" and the "after," the "not yet" and the "already gone" are not to be found in a single painting of the cathedral by Monet. Each painting is depicting the "right now," the hour that is marked on the clock—which, however, Monet chose to blur with paint.[9]

But is Monet's conception (with which we can bracket Riley's) really so original, or at any rate so distinct as a philosophical idea? Do we need an artist to tell us this? A good many writers, besides Newton and myself, have argued for the existence of the "extended subjective present" as a kind of temporal basket in which past, present, and future somehow coalesce. Edmund Husserl, with his idea of the present as a combination of "protention" and "retention" embracing the current "primal impression" [see Figure 24], is the best known; Dan Lloyd, who has recently written a novel around this idea, *Radiant Cool,* may be the most adventurous.[10]

But we should understand that Monet is indeed different. In

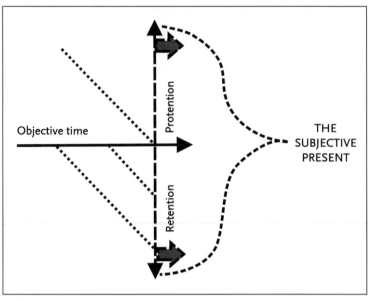

24

contradistinction to what writers who follow Husserl (such as Newton and Lloyd) mean by the subjective present, what Monet is getting
at is much more radical.

The Husserlian idea of *borrowing* from past and future could
be considered quite traditional. For a painter of classical historical
paintings, as Louis Marin has pointed out, "the only possible way of
making the story understood by the viewer, or 'read', is to distribute,
all around his central represented moment, various circumstances
that are logically connected to it by implication or presupposition."[11]

And this is the way our minds typically operate. Blaise Pascal complained: "We never keep to the present. We anticipate the future as if we found it too slow in coming and were trying to hurry it up, or we recall the past as if to stay its too rapid flight. We are so unwise that we wander about in times that do not belong to us, and do not think of the only one that does."[12]

However, Monet breaks with this tradition altogether. As Pissarro notes, Monet really has no interest in "protention" or "retention"; he only wants the "now." Future and past count for nothing as he tries to depict the reality of the eternal present. Thus, what happens in the thick moment of conscious sensation, Monet seems to be suggesting, is *not* that we blend past, present, and future but rather that we take a single moment and *hold on to it just as it is*—so that each moment is experienced *as it happens for longer than it happens.*

I have tried to illustrate this diagrammatically in Figure 25. Each "instantaneous effect" outlives the physical instant, being held in the dimension of subjective time while it fades slowly away, while remaining separate from the next effect. I am not sure the diagram does the idea justice. If you can't say it, you can't easily draw it in two, or even three dimensions (but I do not think this need worry us as a psychological objection—the *mind* is not short of dimensions, even if my computer graphics package is).

So, now, let's return to our task of trying to say what is so special about phenomenal experience. Can the efforts of the artists to con-

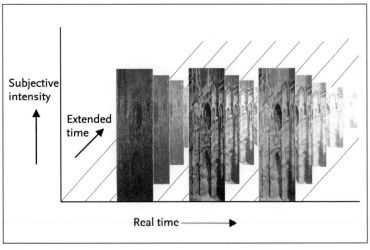

25

vey the nature of sensation provide us with useful insights to inform our science? Suppose, as an exercise in metaphor, we put a painting by Riley or Monet on the right-hand side of the mind-brain identity equation in place of the brain, will the painter's tricks for depicting instantaneity genuinely help?

I think they not only *help,* they go right to the heart of it. So much so that I will say straight out that once we take on board the ideas of *self-similarity, rhyme, and temporal doubling,* then, for the X factor, the game is nearly up.

Nearly. But I have to say not quite. For it must be all too obvious that these ideas still desperately need stabilizing. If only we could now extend a steadying hand over to sensation on the left-hand side, not from painting as a metaphor but from the brain as the real thing. If some kind of paradoxical temporal thickening really is what characterizes the experience of sensation, do we have anything suitable in our model of brain activity to match it with? The brain is not a painting. But does the brain do painting-like things?

Several theorists, coming from different directions, have in fact had the hunch that the key to the special quality of consciousness lies with "re-entrant circuits" in the brain, neural activity that loops back on itself, so as to create some kind of *self-resonance*.[13] But how can this possibly relate to the model we have proposed? How can we get re-entrant feedback out of covert bodily expression? As it happens, I think we can claim the ground has been perfectly prepared by the evolutionary story we sketched in Chapter 4 about the history of those primitive "wriggles of acceptance or rejection."

Let's recap the last stage of this story. We suggested that, as and when the sensory responses become biologically redundant, the sensory responses get *privatized*. The command signals get short-circuited before they reach the body surface, so that instead of reaching all the way out to the peripheral site of stimulation, they now reach only to points more and more central on the incoming sensory pathways, until eventually the whole process becomes closed off from the outside world in an internal loop within the brain [refer back to Figure 20].

But of course this creates precisely the conditions needed for the creation of a feedback loop. Indeed, feedback has been a feature of sensation all along. Ever since the days when sensory responses were actual wriggles at the body surface, these responses have been having feedback effects by modifying the very stimulation to which they are a response. In the early days, however, this feedback circuit would have been too roundabout and slow to have had any interesting consequences. However, as and when the response circuit becomes internalized and the pathway so much shortened, the conditions are certainly there for a significant degree of recursive interaction to come into play [Figure 26].

That's to say, the command signals for sensory responses could well begin to interact with the very input to which they are a response—so as to become partly self-creating and self-sustaining. These signals would still take their cue from input from the body surface, and still get styled by it, but on another level they would indeed have become signals *about themselves.*

It seems we are in luck after all! We have the possibility of something emerging on the brain side that could be just the ticket to support a kind of temporal thickening on the experience side. It seems our model of sensations may be capable of delivering the X factor in just the way we hoped.

Except for one more problem. To get sustained feedback of the kind that is needed to underlie an appropriate level of temporal thickening, there will have to be *very fine tuning*—a precise matching

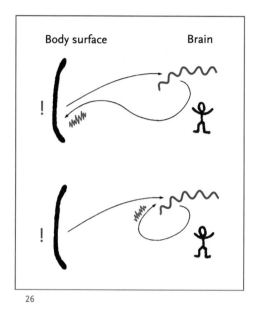

of output with input, so as to provide exactly the right degree of re-inforcement of the signal in the loop. I wrote just now that we have the possibility of something so wonderfully well-tuned "emerging." But do we really want to rely on "emergence" to explain this?

Figure 26 is taken from my book, *A History of the Mind*. In that book I confess I elided this issue. I implied that once the sensory response circuits have evolved to the point where they could in principle support sustained feedback, the rest will follow simply as a matter of course. But the truth is, it is most unlikely to happen automatically. In fact it will not happen unless it is *designed* to happen, and this has to mean, presumably, *designed by natural selection.*

But, why? What ever could be the payoff—the functional, biological payoff—of feedback that brings about a thickening of consciousness? Let me jump right in. I think the payoff is that it gives the subject a quite new sense of Self. *It lifts the subject out of zombiedom.*

In Chapter 2 I drew attention to what Frege said about the Self: "It seems absurd to us that a pain, a mood, a wish should rove about the world without a bearer, independently. An experience is impossible without an experient. The inner world presupposes the person whose inner world it is." Frege's point, as we noted, was that you cannot have experiences until you have got a subject for them. But the point I emphasized was the antithesis of this (or maybe the corollary): You cannot have a subject for experiences until you have got them. That's to say, *a subject has to have something to be the subject of.*

Now, let's follow where I already hinted this was going. I think that this second point is not only just as logical as Frege's, but at a human level potentially far more important. Because, for anyone who reflects on it, it leads, beyond the relatively dull analytic conclusion that "I have such and such experiences therefore I am," to the potentially astonishing revelation that "I am because I have such and such experiences."

I do not mean to imply that most human beings—let alone non-human or prehuman animals—ever articulate any such discovery. Nonetheless, the revelation, however it gets through, that "*This is what it means to be me!*" surely is—or can be—headline news, something with the potential to inspire new forms of self-interest and self-respect.

Now comes the question. Granted that a subject must be the subject *of* something, what kind of thing is up to doing the job? Not all experiences will be of equal value—at any rate not in *this* role. Indeed, I would say that most of the candidate experiences in nature will not fit the bill at all: they simply will not have the *substance*, the *psychic weight*, to provide what it takes to support the existence of a Self.

What *does* it take? What is required of an experience if it is to be such that a subject can proudly be the subject of it? I believe the answer is the very property that we have just now identified as central to the experience of sensation: the substantiality that goes with *existing in thick time*.

A Self that has *this* at its center will be a self to be reckoned with, a self worth having. Such a Self will burst with the potential for natural selection to shape it up still further, so that it can become the organizing principle for each individual's mental life. And the benefits hardly need spelling out. Human beings, as subjects of something so remarkable, gain new confidence and interest in their own personal survival. What's more—and what may well be much more—they come to value conscious selfhood in others too.

But it goes further. Thomas Clark has remarked how consciousness cannot but inflate a person's *metaphysical self-worth:* "It may be that the sorts of higher level cognitive processes which are found to correlate with consciousness inevitably generate (among language users) a self/world model containing the strong intuition that the self and its experience cannot simply be the body, cannot just be a bit of the world suitably organized. Explaining consciousness satisfactorily will consist in overcoming that intuition, and in placing experience fully within the natural, physical realm."[14]

Clark here seems to suggest that the belief in "mind-body duality" is a kind of cognitive illusion, something that "inevitably" emerges as an accidental—and possibly maladaptive—by-product of reflecting on the nature of experience. A mistake which we must try to "overcome." He is correct, presumably, in saying it is an illusion. And he is very likely correct in saying it emerges pretty much "inevitably" from reflection on the facts. However, let us not be so quick to judge it a mistake.

I have a contrary proposal: I dare say belief in mind-body duality may not be "accidental" in the least.

In the wider world, there are two sorts of "illusion"—accidental and contrived. There are cases where we get things wrong as the result of bad luck, and cases where we are the victims of deliberate trickery. When, for example, we see a stick in water as being bent, or when we think we are moving as the train beside us pulls away, it is a matter of bad luck. We are applying rules of inference in situations where our information is inaccurate or incomplete. But no one is *trying* to delude us.

When, however, we see a stage magician bending a metal spoon without touching it, or when we feel the table at a spiritualist seance lifting off the ground, it is a matter of intentional trickery. We may, again, be applying rules of inference in situations where our information is inaccurate or incomplete. But this time there is an illusionist who *wants* us to get it wrong.

Now, with belief in mind-body duality, which kind of illusion is it? The general view among materialist philosophers has always been that it is an illusion of the first kind, an honest—if regrettable—error.[15] But how about if it is actually an illusion of the second kind, a deliberate trick!

Could it be? Only of course if there were to be an active agency behind it, playing the role of the illusionist. But who or what could possibly be doing this? And what interest could they have in encouraging individual humans to believe in a non-physical soul?

The immediate, but unhelpful answer, might be that, since it is a case of self-delusion, the illusionist must lie within the subject's own brain. The more interesting answer might be that, insofar as the brain is designed by genes, the illusionist is the subject's own genes.

But, in that case, the ultimate answer must surely be that the illusionist is Nature herself, working through natural selection.

Suppose that, at a relatively late stage in human evolution, after the thick moment of consciousness has already become firmly established as an anchor for the Self, variant genes arise whose effect is to give the conscious Self just the extra twist that leads the human mind to form an exaggeratedly grandiose view of its own nature. Suppose, in other words, that, while as Clark says "the self and its experience" is and ever will be "just a bit of the world suitably organized," *this* bit of the world becomes reorganized precisely so as to impress the subject with its *out-of-this-world* qualities. Then suppose that those individuals who *are* so impressed, those who fall for the illusion, tend to have longer and more productive lives.

Could it be so? If you promise not to let this final hypothesis overshadow all the other passably good ideas in this book, I will chance my arm and say I think it could be and it is. Indeed, I think that, once we have eyes for it, it is easy to see the belief in mind-body duality operating as a remarkable new biological adaptation at every turn in human natural history.

Time and again what makes the difference—what makes human beings, uniquely among living creatures, so ambitious to succeed, what makes them aim so high for themselves and their children (so improbably, impossibly high), what makes them, in short, the amazing piece of work that humans are—is nothing less than their conviction that as human souls they have something extra-special to preserve, even beyond death.

The philosopher Thomas Nagel has put it like this: "There are elements which, if added to one's experience, make life better; there are other elements which, if added to one's experience make life worse. But what remains when these are set aside is not merely *neutral:* it is emphatically positive . . . The additional positive weight is supplied by experience itself, rather than by any of its contents."[16]

He is right. But because, like moral philosophers in general, he does not look into the evolutionary background, he does not know why he is right.

7

My project in this book, I said at the beginning, was to move toward an explanation of just why consciousness *matters*. A new answer has been showing above the waves, stepping tentatively onto land. Consciousness matters *because it is its function to matter*. It has been designed to create in human beings a Self whose life is worth pursuing.

To start with, the Self is *there* for us, phenomenally thick and substantial. And *being there* is a huge advance on not being there. A temporally-thick Self is something to build a rich subjective life on. But for human beings it may very well go further. For we now have a Self that, however we come to it, seems to inhabit *a different universe of spiritual being*. And this is something else.

My suggestion is that in the course of human evolution, our ancestors who thought of their own consciousness as metaphysically remarkable—existing outside normal space and time—would have taken themselves still more seriously as Selves. The more mysterious and unworldly the qualities of consciousness, the more seriously significant the Self. And the more significant the Self, the greater the boost to human self-confidence and self-importance—and the greater the value that individuals place on their own and others' lives.

In which case it is easy to see how the very qualities of consciousness that seem to render it so mysterious and magical would have been the occasion for consciousness's becoming a runaway evolutionary success. In fact, these qualities would soon have been designed in.

Listen again to the chorus of those commentators who positively revel in their own—and, as they see it, others'—lack of understanding.

> Consciousness is a fascinating but elusive phenomenon; it is impossible to specify what it is, what it does, or why it evolved. Nothing worth reading has been written about it.[1]

> Nobody has the slightest idea how anything material could be conscious. Nobody even knows what it would be like to have the slightest idea about how anything material could be conscious.[2]

> Isn't it perfectly evident to you that . . . [the brain] is just the wrong kind of thing to give birth to [phenomenal] consciousness. You might as well assert that numbers emerge from biscuits or ethics from rhubarb.[3]

The answer with which I will leave you—and them, if they are listening—is: *Yes, that's the point!*

Joe King wrote to me concerning his anxiety about what would happen to him after his death, and his hopes of escaping from his wizened body. I replied, as best I could.

Dear Joe,

You ask whether I think consciousness can survive the death of the brain. It's the most natural of all questions to ask. I think we human beings are *made* to ask it. I even think that in asking it we become better people. But my straight answer, as a scientist, is: *not a chance.* Consciousness is something we do with our brains.

This is both good and bad news. The bad news is obvious. The good news is that each moment of consciousness is, as you already know it is, amazingly precious. Albert Camus wrote, "The present and the succession of presents before a constantly conscious soul is the ideal of the absurd man."[4] But Camus' "absurd man" is both heroic and wise. He recognizes that when we cannot travel the wide sea of eternity, the more significant is the island that we stand on now.

I shall be giving some lectures in Harvard in the Spring, called *Seeing Red.* I wish you could be there. I think you, as a musician, would appreciate the analogy I draw between conscious sensation and a work of art.

But I also copied to Joe King a poem by Gerard Manley Hop-kins—a poem about mirroring, rhyme, resonance, self, self-expres-sion, and doing—that says it all. I hardly dare read it.

> As kingfishers catch fire, dragonflies draw flame;
> As tumbled over rim in roundy wells
> Stones ring; like each tucked string tells, each hung bell's
> Bow swung finds tongue to fling out broad its name;
> Each mortal thing does one thing and the same:
> Deals out that being indoors each one dwells;
> Selves—goes itself; *myself* it speaks and spells,
> Crying What I do is me: for that I came.[5]

NOTES

Chapter 1

1 Thomas Reid to Lord Kames, 1775, in "Unpublished Letters of Thomas Reid to Lord Kames, 1762–1782," ed. Ian S. Ross, *Texas Studies in Literature and Language* 7 (1965): 17–65.

2 Joe King, e-mail to Nicholas Humphrey, 17 Nov. 2003. Joe King's Web page is www.joepking.com.

3 Stuart Sutherland, *The International Dictionary of Psychology* (London: Crossroad, 1989).

4 Thomas Nagel, *The View from Nowhere* (Oxford: Oxford University Press, 1986), p. 4.

5 Nicholas Humphrey, "Seeing Red: A Study in Consciousness"(Mind/Brain/ Behavior Initiative Distinguished Lecture Series, Harvard University, Cambridge, Mass., 19–21 April 2004).

Chapter 2

1 Maurice Bowra, *Memories, 1898–1939* (Cambridge, Mass.: Harvard University Press, 1967).

2 Bridget Riley, "Colour for the Painter," in *Colour: Art and Science*, ed. Trevor Lamb and Janine Bourriau (Cambridge: Cambridge University Press, 1995), pp. 31–64; quotation from p. 31.

3 Helen Vendler, *The Art of Shakespeare's Sonnets* (Cambridge, Mass.: Harvard University Press, 1997), p. 1.

4 Wassily Kandinsky, *Concerning the Spiritual in Art*, trans. M. T. H. Sadler (1911; New York: Dover, 1977), p. 25.

5 Nicholas Humphrey and G. R. Keeble, "Effects of Red Light and Loud Noise on the Rate at which Monkeys Sample Their Sensory Environment," *Perception* 7 (1978): 343–348.

6 Nicholas Humphrey, "The Colour Currency of Nature," in *Colour for Architecture*, ed. Tom Porter and Byron Mikellides (London: Studio-Vista, 1976), pp. 95–98; Nicholas Humphrey, "Colour Is the Keyboard," in *A History of the Mind* (London: Chatto and Windus, 1982), pp. 38–40; John Gage, *Colour and Culture* (London: Thames and Hudson, 1993).

7 Porter and Mikellides, *Colour for Architecture*, p. 12.

8 Richard de Villamil, *Newton the Man* (London: Gordon Knox, 1931), pp. 14–16.

9 Nicholas Humphrey, "Interest and Pleasure: Two Determinants of a Monkey's Visual Preferences," *Perception* 1 (1972): 395–416.

10 Peter Meijer, "Seeing with Sound," *The vOICe*, www.seeingwithsound.com/voice.htm (accessed 2004).

11 D. K. O'Neill, J. W. Astington, and J. H. Flavell, "Young Children's Understanding of the Role Sensory Experience Plays in Knowledge Acquisition," *Child Development* 63 (1992): 474–490.

12 Alexandra Y. Aikhenvald and R. M. W. Dixon, eds., *Studies in Evidentiality* (Amsterdam: John Benjamins, 2003).

13 Gottlob Frege, "The Thought: A Logical Inquiry," in *Philosophical Logic,* ed. P. F. Strawson (1918; Oxford: Oxford University Press, 1967), p. 27.

14 Lord Byron to Annabella Milbanke (later Lady Byron), 1813, quoted in Benjamin Woolley, *The Bride of Science: Romance, Reason and Byron's Daughter* (London: MacMillan, 1999), p. 28.

15 I. C. McManus, Amanda L. Jones, and Jill Cottrell, "The Aesthetics of Colour," *Perception* 10 (1981): 651–666.

16 Nicholas Humphrey, "The Privatization of Sensation," in *Towards a Science of Consciousness III,* ed. S. R. Hameroff, A. W. Kaszniak, and D. J. Chalmers (Cambridge, Mass.: MIT Press, 1999), pp. 247–258; also in Nicholas Humphrey, *The Mind Made Flesh* (Oxford: Oxford University Press, 2002), pp. 115–125.

17 The term "zombie" has a colloquial and, in recent philosophy, more technical meaning. I am using it here to refer to the situation of a subject who lacks phenomenal consciousness—with all that this entails. But I am not using it, in the way that philosophers such as David Chalmers do, to refer to the situation of a subject whose lack of phenomenal consciousness *entails nothing at all.* I believe, along with Daniel Dennett, that this latter idea is incoherent (Dennett, "The Zombic Hunch: Extinction of an Intuition?" in *Philosophy at the New Millennium,* ed. Anthony O'Hear, Royal Institute of Philosophy Supplement 48 (Cambridge: Cambridge University Press, 2001), pp. 27–43). However, it is important that we recognize just what an attractive incoherent idea it is—and how the phenomenon of blindsight provides, as it were, a "near miss" for the state of philosophical zombiedom.

18 Stephen Fry, *Liar* (London: Mandarin, 1992), p. 166.

19 Ludwig Wittgenstein, *Philosophical Investigations, Part II* (Oxford: Blackwell, 1958), p. 212.

Chapter 3

1 Jerry Fodor, "You Can't Argue with a Novel," *London Review of Books*, 4 March 2004, p. 31.

2 Daniel Dennett, *Kinds of Minds* (New York: Basic Books, 1996), p. 67.

3 Thomas Reid, *Essays on the Intellectual Powers of Man*, part 2, ch. 17 (1785; Cambridge, Mass.: MIT Press, 1969), p. 265.

4 Reid, *Intellectual Powers*, part 2, ch. 16, p. 242.

5 Reid, *Intellectual Powers*, part 2, ch. 16, p. 243.

6 Described in a series of papers, beginning with N. K. Humphrey and L. Weiskrantz, "Vision in Monkeys after Removal of the Striate Cortex," *Nature* 215 (1967): 595–597; ending with Nicholas Humphrey, "Vision in a Monkey without Striate Cortex: A Case Study," *Perception* 3 (1974): 241–255.

7 In studying the visual-responses of single cells in the sub-cortical visual system of monkeys, I had found evidence that this "primitive" system, which remains intact after removal of the visual cortex, might be capable of supporting quite finely-tuned visually guided behavior. N. K. Humphrey, "Responses to Visual Stimuli of Single Units in the Superior Colliculus of Rats and Monkeys," *Experimental Neurology* 20 (1968): 312–340.

8 Nicholas Humphrey, "Seeing and Nothingness," *New Scientist* 53 (1972): 682–684.

9 Lawrence Weiskrantz, *Blindsight* (Oxford: Clarendon, 1986).

10 Petra Stoerig and Alan Cowey, "Wavelength Discrimination in Blindsight," *Brain* 115 (1992): 425–444.

11 MacDonald Critchley, *The Parietal Lobes* (London: Hafner, 1966), p. 299.

12 In S. Cohen, *Drugs of Hallucination: The Uses and Misuses of LSD* (London: Secker and Warburg, 1964), p. 16.

13 Stephen M. Kosslyn, 1987. [Kosslyn confirms that he wrote this, but neither he nor I have been able to track down the original source. However, he makes a briefer observation to the same effect in a later paper: "In some of these patients object identification apparently is not dramatically disrupted." S. M. Kosslyn, R. A. Flynn, J. B. Amsterdam, and G. Wang, "Components of High-Level Vision: A Cognitive Neuroscience Analysis and Accounts of Neurological Syndromes," *Cognition* 34 (1990): 203–277; quotation from p. 263].

14 This is an improved version of the model I put forward in *A History of the Mind* (London: Chatto and Windus, 1992).

15 J. M. Oxbury, S. M. Oxbury, and N. K. Humphrey, "Varieties of Colour Anomia," *Brain* 92 (1969): 847–860.

16 Paul Bach-y-Rita, *Brain Mechanisms in Sensory Substitution* (London: Academic Press, 1972).

17 J. K. O'Regan, E. Myin, and A. Noë, "Skill, Corporality, and Alerting Capacity in an Account of Sensory Consciousness," http://nivea.psycho.univ-paris5.fr/CONS+COG/CC_OREGAN.htm (accessed June 2003), p. 12.

18 Bach-y-Rita, *Brain Mechanisms,* p. 107.

19 www.seeingwithsound.com/voice.htm.

20 Peter Meijer, "Seeing with Sound for the Blind: Is It Vision?," (presentation, Tucson Conference on Consciousness, 8 April 2002), http://www.seeingwithsound.com/tucson2002.html.

21 In Lakshmi Sandhana, "Blind 'See' with Sound," *BBC News,* http://news.bbc.co.uk/1/hi/sci/tech/3171226.stm (accessed 13 Oct. 2003).

22 O'Regan, Myin, and Noë, "Skill, Corporality," p. 12.

23 "What Blind Users Say about the vOICe," *The vOICe*, www.seeingwith sound.com/voice.htm.

24 Daniel Dennett, "It's Not a Bug, It's a Feature," *Journal of Consciousness Studies* 7 (2000): 25–27; quotation from p. 25.

25 Colin McGinn, review of "A History of the Mind," *London Review of Books*, 10 October 1992.

26 Robert van Gulick, "Closing the Gap," *Journal of Consciousness Studies* 7 (2000): 93–97; quotation from p. 95.

27 Valerie Hardcastle, "Hard Things Made Hard," *Journal of Consciousness Studies* 7 (2000): 51–53; quotation from p. 52.

28 Peter Rigby, cartoon in *Prospect*, January 2004, p. 45. Reprinted by permission of the artist.

29 Reid, *Intellectual Powers*, part 2, ch. 17, p. 265.

30 K. Carrie Armel and V. S. Ramachandran, "Projecting Sensations to External Objects: Evidence from Skin Conductance Response," *Proceedings of the Royal Society of London: Biological* 270 (2003): 1499–1506. Figure reprinted by permission.

31 MacDonald Critchley has described a curious illusion, which now perhaps makes sense. "A remarkable dissociation between color and object has been described after central lesions to the visual system . . . Colours may seem to be 'loosened' from the confines of their objects so as to constitute a 'separation of color from the object.' . . . As colours no longer appear to be integral to the objects in question, they may seem to occupy a plane somewhere between the subject and the object . . . When the patient wishes to touch something, he has an odd impression as though he had to plunge his hand through a translucent sheet." MacDonald Critchley, "Acquired Anomalies of

Colour Perception of Central Origin," *Brain* 88 (1965): 711–724; quotation from p. 719.

32 There are reviews of blindsight by Weiskrantz, *Blindsight;* Petra Stoerig and Alan Cowey, "Blindsight in Man and Monkey," *Brain* 120 (1997): 535–559; Anthony J. Marcel, "Blindsight and Shape Perception: Deficit of Visual Consciousness or of Visual Function?" *Brain* 121 (1998): 1565–1588. See also specific references below.

33 Petra Stoerig, "Varieties of Vision: From Blind Responses to Conscious Recognition," *Trends in Neurosciences* 19 (1996): 401–406.

34 L. Weiskrantz, "Introduction: Dissociated Issues," in *The Neuropsychology of Consciousness,* ed. A. D. Milner and M. D. Rugg (London: Academic Press, 1991), pp. 1–10; quotation from p. 8.

35 This possibility is raised explicitly in Nicholas Humphrey, "Nature's Psychologists," in *Consciousness and the Physical World,* ed. B. Josephson and V. S. Ramachandran (Oxford: Pergamon, 1980), pp. 57–75; reprinted in Nicholas Humphrey, *Consciousness Regained* (Oxford: Oxford University Press, 1983), pp. 29–41.

36 C. Ackroyd, N. K. Humphrey, and E. K. Warrington, "Lasting Effects of Early Blindness: A Case Study," *Quarterly Journal of Experimental Psychology* 26 (1974): 114–124.

37 Ibid., p. 116.

Chapter 4

1 Francis Crick and Christof Koch, "A Framework for Consciousness," *Nature Neuroscience* 6 (2003): 119–126; quotation from p. 119.

2 John Searle, "Consciousness: What We Still Don't Know," review of *The*

Quest for Consciousness, by Christof Koch, *New York Review of Books,* 13 Jan. 2005, p. 36.

3 The next three paragraphs are taken from Nicholas Humphrey, "How to Solve the Mind-Body Problem," *Journal of Consciousness Studies* 7 (2000): 5–20.

4 A. S. Ramsey, *Dynamics* (Cambridge: Cambridge University Press, 1954), p. 42.

5 Colin McGinn, "Consciousness and Cosmology: Hyperdualism Ventilated," in *Consciousness,* ed. M. Davies and G. W. Humphreys (Oxford: Blackwell, 1993), pp. 155–177; quotation from p. 160.

6 Natika Newton, "Emergence and the Uniqueness of Consciousness," *Journal of Consciousness Studies* 8 (2001): 47–59; quotation from p. 48.

7 Much of what follows in this chapter was given its first airing in Nicholas Humphrey, *A History of the Mind* (London: Chatto and Windus, 1992). The argument was further developed in Humphrey, "Mind-Body Problem" (from which some paragraphs are taken). But I have added here several new ideas.

8 The story that follows imagines there to have been continuities in the way organisms experience the world, across vast time spans and levels of biological organization, which I realize are biologically quite implausible. Still, even as we acknowledge that this is not literally what happened, let's note that unlikely continuities have been a reality in evolution. New evidence about overlapping genomes shows that the same genes continue to play the same functional role in widely separated organisms, despite huge twists and turns in evolutionary history and even entirely new beginnings. Thus, for example, the Pax 6 gene that determines the development of the eye in fruit-flies is involved in determining the development of the eye in mammals—even though the eyes of flies and mammals are constructed on quite different

principles (if the Pax-6 from a mouse is translated into a fly, it directs the formation of an additional compound insect eye). Still more to the point, in relation to the evolution of sensation, from amoeba to human, Lynn Margulis has recently claimed that "our ability to perceive signals in the environment evolved directly from our bacterial ancestors [sic]." See www.edge.org/q2005/q05_7.html#margulis.

9 The footprints are on a slab of shale, at the foot of a sea-cliff on Valentia Island, County Kerry. On this occasion the footprints had been filled in with milk by mourners following the funeral of a local fisherman.

Chapter 5

1 Friedrich Nietzsche, *The Gay Science,* trans. Walter Kaufmann (1887; New York: Vintage, 1974), p. 298.

2 Friedrich Nietzsche, "Daybreak," in *A Nietzsche Reader,* ed. and trans. R. J. Hollingdale (1881; Harmondsworth: Penguin, 1977), p. 156.

3 Stephanie D. Preston and Frans B. M. de Waal, "Empathy: Its Ultimate and Proximate Bases," *Behavioral and Brain Sciences* 25 (2002): 1–72.

4 G. Rizzolatti, L. Fogassi, and V. Gallese, "Neurophysiological Mechanisms Underlying the Understanding and Imitation of Action," *Nature Reviews Neuroscience* 2 (2001): 661–670.

5 W. D. Hutchison, K. D. Davis, A. M. Loxzno, R. R. Tasker, and J. O. Dostrovsky, "Pain-Regulated Neurons in the Human Cingulate Cortex," *Nature Neuroscience* 2 (1999): 403–405.

6 The question of how mirror neurons for *action* could be involved in empathy for *sensations* is raised in Philip L. Jackson, Andrew N. Meltzoff, and Jean Decety, "How Do We Perceive the Pain of Others? A Window into the Neural Processes Involved in Empathy," *Neuroimage* 24 (2005): 771–779. However,

since it has not occurred to these authors to think of sensations *as* actions, they conclude that mirror neurons are probably not involved: "It constrains their involvement in many everyday empathic situations" (p. 777).

7 Adam Smith, *The Theory of Moral Sentiments,* ed. D. Raphael and A. Macfie (1759; Oxford: Clarendon, 1976), p. 9.

8 J. L. Bradshaw and J. B. Mattingley, "Allodynia: A Sensory Analogue of Motor Mirror Neurons in a Hyperesthetic Patient Reporting Instantaneous Discomfort to Another's Perceived Sudden Minor Injury?" *Journal of Neurology, Neurosurgery and Psychiatry* 70 (2001): 135–136; quotation from p. 136.

9 Michel de Montaigne, *Essays,* ed. and trans. J. M. Cohen, bk. 1, ch. 1 (1572; Harmondsworth: Penguin, 1958), p. 36.

10 Susanne Langer, *Mind: An Essay on Human Feeling, Vol. 3* (Baltimore: Johns Hopkins University Press, 1984).

11 However, let's note that this way of explaining empathy for sensations is not going to work for *every* kind of mental state. It works to explain the sharing of sensation just because sensations are something the subject *does*—S *does* the redding. But by the same token it will not work for the sharing of propositional attitudes such as perceptions or beliefs, because these are not things the subject *does*—S does not *do* his perception that the screen is colored red. So, while our model provides strong support for the idea that people may easily and naturally *simulate* another's *sensations,* it would seem likely that people still need a *theory* to enter the world of other people's *thoughts.*

Chapter 6

1 Robert Pirsig, *Zen and the Art of Motorcycle Maintenance* (London: Bodley Head, 1974), p. 13.

2 Natika Newton, "Emergence and the Uniqueness of Consciousness," *Journal of Consciousness Studies* 8 (2001): 47–59; quotation from p. 55.

3 Nicholas Humphrey, *A History of the Mind* (London: Chatto and Windus, 1992): p. 170.

4 Natika Newton, "Emergence," p. 51.

5 F. P. Ramsey, "General Propositions and Causality," in *F. P. Ramsey: Philosophical Papers,* ed. D. H. Mellor (Cambridge: Cambridge University Press, 1990), p. 146.

6 Henry Sidgwick, *Methods of Ethics* (London: MacMillan, 1874), p. 190.

7 *Bridget Riley: 26 June–28 September 2003,* exhibition catalogue (London: Tate Gallery, 2003), www.tate.org.uk/britain/exhibitions/riley.

8 Metropolitan Museum of Art, "European Paintings: Work 1944 of 2307," *Works of Art: The Metropolitan Museum of Art,* permanent collection catalogue, www.metmuseum.org/Works_Of_Art.

9 Joachim Pissarro, *Monet's Cathedral* (London: Pavilion, 1990): p. 22.

10 For an overview of Husserl's views, and an up-to-date interpretation, see Francisco J. Varela, "The Specious Present: A Neurophenomenology of Time Consciousness," in *Naturalizing Phenomenology: Issues in Contemporary Phenomenology and Cognitive Science,* ed. J. Petitot, F. J. Varela, J.-M. Roy, and B. Pachoud (Stanford: Stanford University Press, 1999), pp. 266–314. Dan Lloyd, *Radiant Cool* (Cambridge, Mass.: Bradford, 2003).

11 Louis Marin, *Towards a Theory of Reading* (Cambridge: Calligram, 1988), p. 67.

12 Blaise Pascal, *Pensées,* trans. A. J. Krailsheimer (1669; Harmondsworth: Penguin, 1966), 1.47.

13 For reviews, see Daniel A. Pollen, "On the Neural Correlates of Visual Perception," *Cerebral Cortex* 9 (1999): 4–19; Daniel A. Pollen, "Explicit Neural Representations, Recursive Neural Networks and Conscious Visual Perception," *Cerebral Cortex* 13 (2003): 807–814; Varela, "Specious Present"; Lloyd, *Radiant Cool.*

14 Thomas W. Clark, "Function and Phenomenology: Closing the Explanatory Gap," *Journal of Consciousness Studies* 2 (1995): 241–254; quotation from p. 254.

15 Daniel Dennett, for example, pities his mysterian colleagues for imagining that consciousness is some kind of non-functional add-on to the mind which could in principle be separated from it (the "zombic hunch," Dennett calls this), but implies that the mistake is understandable and correctable. See Dennett, "The Zombic Hunch: Extinction of an Intuition?" in *Philosophy at the New Millenium,* ed. Anthony O'Hear, Royal Institute of Philosophy Supplement 48 (Cambridge: Cambridge University Press, 2001), pp. 27–43.

16 Thomas Nagel, *Mortal Questions* (Cambridge: Cambridge University Press, 1979), p. 2.

Chapter 7

1 Stuart Sutherland, *The International Dictionary of Psychology* (London: Crossroad, 1989).

2 Jerry Fodor, "The Big Idea: Can There Be a Science of Mind?" *Times Literary Supplement* 3 (July 1992): 5.

3 Colin McGinn, "Consciousness and Cosmology: Hyperdualism Ventilated," in *Consciousness,* ed. M. Davies and G. W. Humphreys (Oxford: Blackwell, 1993), pp. 155–177.

4 Albert Camus, *The Myth of Sisyphus,* trans. Justin O'Brien (1942; New York: Knopf, 1955), p. 63.

5 G. M. Hopkins, "As Kingfishers Catch Fire," in *Poems* (London: Humphrey Milford, 1918).

ACKNOWLEDGMENTS

John Maynard Keynes wrote (in the introduction to his *General Theory*): "It is astonishing what foolish things one can temporarily believe if one thinks too long alone." I confess that several of the central ideas in this book have been developed on my own. Indeed, I have to some degree deliberately kept myself separate from the mainstream of cognitive science. The reader will judge whether the result is foolish or not. But I'll say this in my defense: Seeing how so many clever people in the field have made zero progress with the hard problem of consciousness, there is something to be said for staying apart—if not aloof.

I'm happy to say Daniel Dennett has always been there for me, as have Arien Mack and Anthony Marcel. Keith Sutherland published an earlier version of my theory and put together an excellent panel of commentators in the *Journal of Consciousness Studies* 7 (2000). John Brockman brought it to the attention of the EDGE community and generated a spirited discussion (http://www.edge.org/3rd_culture/humphrey04/humphrey04_index.htm).

But my chief debt, in relation to this book, is to the board of the Mind, Brain and Behavior Initiative at Harvard, who invited me to give the Distinguished Lecture Series in 2004. They cannot have foreseen quite what they were getting. Elizabeth Knoll, at Harvard University Press, saw it and didn't blink. More thanks to her.

INDEX